BISHOP FOR A DAY
IDEAS TO HEAL AND RENEW THE CATHOLIC CHURCH

REVEREND DOCTOR
RONALD P. POPIVCHAK

INFINITY
PUBLISHING

ISBN 978-1-4958-0484-7
ISBN 978-1-4958-0485-4 eBook

Published January 2015

INFINITY PUBLISHING
1094 New DeHaven Street, Suite 100
West Conshohocken, PA 19428-2713
Toll-free (877) BUY BOOK
Local Phone (610) 941-9999
Fax (610) 941-9959
Info@buybooksontheweb.com
www.buybooksontheweb.com

DEDICATION

We dedicate this modest work to Holy Father Francis, the Bishop of Rome, and to Archbishop Stefan, the Ukrainian Catholic Metropolitan of Philadelphia, and to all the good bishops of the USA in their combined effort to heal and renew the Church. We also remember in gratitude our late parents Peter and Martha, who taught us about life, and the late Father Russell Danylchuck, who taught us all about the priestly life of service to our brothers and sisters in the Lord Jesus the Christ.

Reverend Dr. Ronald Popivchak

CONTENTS

BISHOP FOR A DAY

As of January 1, 2012, there were 72 Diocesan Archbishops and 373 Diocesan Bishops serving both the Latin and Eastern Catholic Churches in the USA. These 445 Prelates are called upon to serve some 68 million faithful, about 22% of the American population. And they have one of the toughest jobs in the world of religion.

The greatest problem in recent years has been the public relations nightmare stemming from the child abuse scandal. As the Prelates strive mightily to navigate a course between loyalty to their priests and devotion to their young charges, they frequently are pilloried both in the press and the pews for siding with one party or the other. Some Prelates have been removed, others resigned and the rest soldier on in hope and trepidation. All told, more than 3 billion dollars has been paid out, in people's money, to victims, courts and lawyers as a result of this scandal.

Many Dioceses have serious financial problems, some even ending up in bankruptcy court. Much of the financial short-fall is due to the abuse scandal, but some is due to simple mismanagement.

And then there are the problems of the shortage of priests, the closing of parishes, the loss of credibility, the lack of fiscal candor and transparency, the decrease of vocations. And looming on the near horizon is the whole panoply of "family" issues to be faced, such as same-sex marriage, remarriage of divorced Catholics, co-habitation of pre-marital couples, birth control and abortion. The USA Bishops are faced with some Olympian challenges today.

However, the helping hand of Divine Providence, in the person of newly elected Pope Francis, is now reaching out to not only the USA Hierarchs but also to the 4,872 bishops of the world. The Argentinian Pope convoked a Bishops' Synod in the fall of 2014 on the theme of Family Life. And, most remarkably, he asked for the written opinion of the bishops, priests and laity on a whole host of family matters, such as those mentioned above. For the first time in modern history, the Holy Father wants to know what we the priests and you the laity think about the thorny issues of family life! Divine Providence, indeed!

And if the Pope himself wants ideas, far be it from me to refuse this invitation. But I write not only out of obligation, but mainly out of love for the faithful and respect for the bishops. And I write as a Pastor with decades of experience with the sole purpose of helping the Church and her betroubled leaders in these difficult times.

If you are curious about my credentials, let me mention just a few. I have been a priest two years longer than the Pope, many years longer than most bishops. I have been a parish priest in five churches, from a Cathedral to a tiny farm town. And I served as Vicar General, Editor of the Archdiocesan newspaper, Director of Vocations, Dean of ten Parishes. I hold a doctorate in Sacred Theology (STD, 1975) from The Catholic University of America. And I write for various publications, most recently The Cambridge History of Christianity.

Several chapters in this work concern family life, such as birth control, abortion, and women in the church. Other chapters discuss problematic issues such as vocations and missions. But all the topics tackle head-on real and difficult matters facing the Church and her leaders, the Bishops, in this Country today. Certainly, if the Holy Father Francis is any guide, these issues are front and center throughout the global Church.

I can only hope and pray that the ideas (even solutions) contained in this modest work will be of some benefit to our church leaders in their role and sacred mission to inspire and guide us all, lay and cleric, in the 21st century.

Rev. Dr. R. P. Popivchak

Note: All the statistics in the INTRODUCTION were taken from "The Catholic Almanac", Our Sunday Visitor Publishing Division, 2012.

CHAPTER I

THE MISSIONS

Virtually all great companies and institutions today have what is known as a "Mission Statement", a brief but pointed affirmation of their main purpose in life. The Catholic Church was given her mission statement some two millennia ago by Jesus Christ Himself: "Go, therefore, make disciples of all nations; baptize them in the name of the Father and of the Son and of the Holy Spirit, and teach them to observe all the commands I have given you. And know that I am with you always; yes, to the end of time." (Mt. 28:18-20)

The Apostles took this mission statement, this Great Commission, both seriously and literally. Peter and Paul travelled to Antioch and Rome, Andrew to Greece and modern-day Ukraine, Mark to Egypt, Thomas to India, John to Asia Minor. And so it went with all the others. The Apostles, their disciples and successors, now known as Bishops, were so fervently devoted to Christ's command that in less than 300 years the entire Roman Empire was becoming Christianized.

Down through centuries the Christian missionaries have brought the teaching of Christ to the farthest corners of the world. The bishops commissioned individuals such as

St. Patrick (Ireland) and the monk Augustine (England) to be missionaries to the unbaptized. And they commissioned religious orders such as the Jesuits (India and Japan) and Franciscans (the Americas) to open up missions. These and so many other both individuals and religious communities have written a glorious chapter in the history of the Church, not only in ink, but often in their own blood.

Bishops today have a tough enough job directing their diocese or archdiocesan. But they have the additional duty of sharing in the guidance of the Universal Church. They perform this latter task by gathering and deliberating in conferences and synods with other bishops. They often send funds and supplies to missionary outposts in their region. And they even send personnel, both lay and religious, if at all possible, to missions. But it is becoming increasingly difficult, if not impossible, to send such human help to the missions. You simply cannot give what you don't have.

The Maryknoll Society, based in Ossining, NY, has been doing missionary work in Central America since 1943. These priests, brothers and sisters have done heroic work among the Mayans of Guatemala, and the indigenous people of Honduras, El Salvador, Costa Rica and Nicaragua. Maryknoll lay missioners joined this effort in the 1970's. Originally known as the Catholic Foreign Missions Society of America, Maryknoll was established in 1911 as the foreign arm of the American Catholic Church. Literally hundreds of priests, brothers, sisters and laity, all Maryknollers, have served in Central America the last 70 years.

But times have changed. Former Maryknoller Lawrence A. Egan wrote in 2012: "Over the next five years, barring some miraculous change, the Society (of Maryknoll) will most likely have no members left in Central America. Almost all the current members will be in their late seventies or early eighties...If that is what happens – if Maryknoll folds its tent – then the three groups (Priests, brothers, laity) can look back on a job well done."

We chose the Maryknoll Society as an example of the current status of the Church's missionary effort in the Western Hemisphere. This Society, which engaged in the largest missionary labor in the Americas, was founded in1911 to assist the USA Church and Bishops in carrying out the mandate of Jesus Christ. And now this Apostolic effort is dying on the vine. What are the USA Churches, the USA Bishops to do? Is there no hope? Is the missionary effort of the US Catholic Church over and done with? Perhaps not. There still may be hope.

The various Evangelical Churches have found a way to do very successful mission work in Mexico and Central America, the closest mission lands to the lower Forty-eight of the USA. And so has the Church of the Latter Day Saints, the Mormons. For example, about 8% of all Mexicans belong to the various Evangelical Churches – some 9 million people. As many as 20% of all Guatemalans are Evangelical, some 2.8 million people. Some 18% of Hondurans have recently become Evangelical, about 1.5 million people. Brazil's population numbers about 15% Evangelical faithful, more than 31 million members! Not very long ago these countries and their neighbors were 99% Catholic!

The most recent data from Latin America indicate a dramatic lessening of a Catholic presence in the region. The Pew Research Center reported (USA TODAY, Nov. 14, 2014) that only 69% of Latin Americans now regard themselves as Catholics. About 19% call themselves Protestant-Evangelical, while 8% define themselves as agnostics or unaffiliated. The report concluded that the most common reason for leaving the

Catholic Church was the desire for a more personal connection with God.

How did these Protestant denominations, and to a much lesser extent, the Mormons accomplish this herculean missionary effort in a generation or two? It's simple. They employed lay missionaries. College students, married couples, retirees were dispatched to the mission lands by their religious superiors to preach and teach their version of Christianity. The USA Catholic Church can easily do the same.

There are 235 Catholic colleges and universities in the USA with about 800,000 students, as of 2012. These academic institutions have schools and departments of language (Spanish), medicine, nursing, engineering, religion, international law and business. And all these schools provide their students with lengthy winter and spring breaks! Some 800,000 potential missionaries! Just think what the Evangelicals would do with such an army of possible missionaries!

There is no attempt here to reinvent the wheel. Many Catholic Schools already have in place programs on brief missionary forays into the local urban ghetto, perhaps to Appalachian hollows, Native American reservations, even to Central American outposts. For example, Neumann University, a school in the Franciscan Tradition with a student population of about 3000 some 25 miles west of Philadelphia, has an inspiring program. This School sends about 30 nursing and education students every year to Ecuador, a dozen or so to Camden, NJ and the inner city, as well as a group to Wyoming. These efforts need to be widely publicized and lauded, reported out and increased. But such great service programs could and should be a part of the curriculum of every Catholic college and university in the USA.

We do not advocate nor envision the Bishops operating or overseeing such missionary projects. The Schools are more than well equipped to fulfill such tasks. But we do foresee the Hierarchs encouraging the schools in their jurisdictions to undertake such missions. The bishops have at their disposal a unique and extensive network of connections throughout all the Americas. They can easily determine which brother bishops need support, whether religious, medical, engineering or pure and simple morale. And who better to provide all this than a veritable army of young, strong and bright collegians, some 800,000 in number, to the pockets of poverty, hunger and unbaptized in North and South America?

There is no illusion here that mission work is easy, speedily done or even guaranteed of success. But we are reminded of the words of Don Rumsfeld: "you fight the war with the soldiers you have, not the ones you wish you had." Our old soldiers are in rest homes or cemeteries. The future lies with the young and the brave and the willing. On-the-job training will have to suffice.

Just imagine this scenario. The local bishop goes to the International Airport this spring to see off his Catholic collegians on their mission, a two-week stay in an Appalachian hollow or urban ghetto or even a Central America outpost. The Bishop brings along a crate of supplies; rosaries, missals, Bibles and catechisms for the mission. And the Hierarch even has a modest stipend for all the young missionaries and their adult advisors-professors. And then the Bishop asks all to kneel while he blesses and commissions all the participants. Can you imagine the joy in heaven, the excitement of the students, the pride of their parents, the powerful PR photos in the newspapers? Can you imagine?

And then imagine this scene. At the next meeting of the conference of Catholic Bishops the President asks for a roll-call report on the missions from every Hierarch present. And one by one, from Alabama to Wyoming, the Prelates stand and deliver: 200 collegians to Appalachia, 400 students to the Inner City, 600 missioners to Central America and on it goes. The applause begins and becomes deafening, as handshakes and smiles of pride fill the hotel Conference Hall. The missionary spirit of the Church is back and booming.

And finally let's imagine the scene at the common room of the Maryknollers in Ossining, NY, as the aged and sickly priests and brothers gather around the TV and take in the Bishops' meeting on EWTV. The now retired missionaries in the Rest Home can't believe their weakened eyes and ears! Their work has not been in vain! Their life's work is bearing new fruit. The Church is alive again in the Americas! Thanks to all the Bishops of the USA and their army of young and strong collegians, 800.000 and growing!

There is something powerful and Christ-like happening today on the campuses of the Catholic Schools in the USA. It's time the world took note.

Notes:

"Maryknoll in Central America, 1943-2011", Lawrence A. Egan, Self Published, 2012, p. 157.

All the statistical data were taken from "Our Sunday Visitor's Catholic Almanac", 2012.

CHAPTER II

ABORTION

O f all the issues and problems vexing the Bishops today, abortion is right at the top of the list. Ever since the landmark 1973 decision of the US Supreme Court (Roe v. Wade), which legalized abortion under certain circumstances, the Bishops have been leading the battle in the "abortion wars" across the USA. Yet public opinion and statistics indicate that the battle is near or at a stalemate.

Minnesota Citizens Concerned for Life reports that the number of abortions in the US peaked in 1990 at about 1.6 million. The number has gradually declined since then to reach a total of 1.2 million in 2012. The state-by-state figures reflect this trend. Pennsylvania, for example, reached its peak in 1980 with about 66,000 abortions and declined to about 35,000 in 2012.

It is more than likely that socio-economic circumstances have greatly contributed to these numbers. Some 73% of abortion patients said they simply cannot afford to bear a child or gave a similar reason according to the same survey of the "Minnesota Citizens." A direct correlation between hard economic times and abortion rates can be found in the

Pennsylvania statistics. During the recent "Great Recession" the number of abortions increased from about 35,000 in 2005 to 39,000 in 2008. As the economy improved, the abortion rate fell to about 35,000 in 2012.

The Catholic Church and her Bishops have some strong allies in the anti-abortion struggle. The Evangelical Churches, especially the Baptist branches, as well as the Orthodox Jewish and Islamic communities all side with their Catholic brethren. However, some 68% of Americans still think abortion should be legal in some circumstances, although some 79% do not favor the current abortion-on-demand policy.

Both sides in this abortion issue have chosen their call-names wisely. The anti-abortion side is known as the Pro Life movement. Who could be against "Life"? And the pro-abortion side is called Pro Choice. And who would oppose free choice? Every American loves "Life" and the freedom to make a "choice"! When asked in various polls where they stood, Pro-Life or Pro-Choice, the 2009 totals showed the former at 51% and the latter at 42% among random Americans. Is this progress for the Pro-Life movement or a polling aberration? These polls were published by the Operation Rescue movement, a strong pro-life group.

A serious underlying problem facing the pro-life Catholic Church and her leadership today is that their teaching on abortion places them between two powerful forces in American society. On the one hand is the preservation of life at all costs attitude we see daily with the firemen, police, doctors and nurses. Life is precious for Americans and it simply must be saved. On the other, there is afoot, not only in the USA but throughout the Western World, an equally powerful force known generically as the women's rights movement. Women today are becoming CEOs of major corporations, outnumbering men in law and medical school, even becoming deacons and priests in some Protestant denominations. And these women are not going to be dictated to, especially by male clergy, in personal and private matters such as childbearing. Contemporary women want, even demand, their right to choose.

The Catholic Church is in an especially tough spot here, for her historical record on women's rights is not exactly stellar. A few decades ago it was commonplace to hear from the pulpit that a woman's place was in the home. And it's only been a few years since female altar-servers were allowed in the sanctuary. In a word, the Church cannot allow her anti-abortion stance to be interpreted as anti-women.

It is disturbing, and rightly so, for Church leaders and the laity that as many as 1.2 million abortions per annum are currently being performed in the USA. What should be even more disturbing to all is that 27%, some 324,000 abortions are performed annually for Catholic women. The Protestant totals are even higher with 42% of the 1.2 million abortions in the USA, as reported by Operation Rescue.

The racial breakdown of these same abortion statistics shows that white women abort at a rate of 34% of the 1.2 million in the USA, while black women are at 37%. An alarming note here is that Hispanic women, 85% of whom are Catholic, have 264,000 abortions a year, some 22% of the total, reports Operation Rescue. It is interesting to note that Planned Parenthood, the largest provider of abortions in the USA, has located 80% of its clinics in the minority sections of the large cities of the USA.

New York State is a good example. The city of New York, seat of the powerful and well-resourced Archdiocese of New York, was reported as having 74,658 abortions in 2011 by the

NY Health Department. The entire rest of the New York State reported out 28,020 abortions.

The State of Pennsylvania is home to two large Metropolitan regions: Allegheny County with Pittsburgh as its seat and center and Philadelphia County centered in the same-named City. Wm. Robert Johnston reported in 2012 that these two urban areas accounted for 63% of all PA abortions in 2010.

The Illinois Department of Public Health reported in 2012 that 43,203 abortions were undergone in the state. Cook County, the home of the Chicago Archdiocese, was listed as the site of 24,899 abortions, more than 57% of the entire state.

To complete the statistical analysis of the US abortion scene it should be noted that women in the 20-24 years-of-age group undergo more procedures than any other age grouping, about 33%. Teenagers in the 15-19 age-bracket receive about 17% of the abortions, while women aged 25-29 have 24% of US abortions. Operation Rescue reported this data in 2012.

It is also important to note that about 40% of abortion patients have a family income between $30,000 and less than $15,000 in the USA, close to or deeply in the standard government poverty level. Another 40% of abortion sufferers have a family income between $30,000 and $60,000, according to Operation Rescue. In essence, about half of US abortions are performed on women at or near poverty.

From all the above it is fairly clear that abortion, as a medical procedure and moral choice, is largely confined to the women of the metropolitan centers of the USA, especially those of a racial minority with very limited resources. These women are young in age, 15-25, and lack not only financial support, but also that of a nuclear family structure.

Approximately one-third of all abortions are performed for unmarried women.

It is also clear to this observer that nobody "likes" abortions. Not the vast majority of obstetricians and midwives, not society as a whole, and certainly not the patients themselves. Women get abortions out of desperation and "necessity". They feel they have no other choice, no way out, and no alternative.

The anti-abortion movement is peopled by both large and small organizations. Fr. Rodney Kneifl founded the Servants of the Heart of the Father in Platte Center, NE to urge all God-fearing faithful to pray and fast to end abortions in the USA. Located in the heart of the Archdiocese of Omaha, this modest-sized ministry calls for all to renew "their respect for all people, especially the unborn."

Among the large international groups devoted to ending abortions is the Knights of Columbus, headquartered in New Haven, CT. This million-man organization was founded in New Haven, CT in 1892 by Fr. Michael McGivney as a Catholic fraternal society to aid the Church. It has been active in recent decades as a powerful pro-life force with funds, manpower, publications and programs. For example, since 2009 the Knights have provided $8.5 million to purchase 334 ultrasound machines for use in pro-life clinics through-out the USA.

But the front-line soldiers in the war on abortion have been the private, grass-roots organizations scattered in and around the city. Both stand-alone and branched offices, these groups provide multiple services to pregnant women of all ages, races, colors and creeds. The services vary from a modest food and medical stipend to ultrasound and housing provisions. The Philadelphia Archdiocese on its social services website lists 18 such pro-life offices in its region. But the same website strangely warns that "the Archdiocese does not support, recommend, warrant or guarantee any services offered by the following providers."

The most well-known and largest of these service providers is Birthright, which has four offices in the Philadelphia region. It provides such services as pregnancy testing, ultrasound, examinations, help with medical insurance and even a network of adoption agencies. Birthright's resources come from local volunteers and parishioners, as well as the area Knights of Columbus.

The US Conference of Catholic Bishops (USCCB) has been active in the pro-life battle, mainly in its teaching ministry. The Conference has produced and published several booklets in recent years promoting the pro-life gospel, such as "Life-Giving Love in the Age of Technology" (2009) and "Ethical and Religious Directives" (2009). These exhortative and explanatory pamphlets have been disseminated throughout the USA Catholic parishes. One might assume, however, that most Catholics already know that abortion is a terrible and tragic choice.

Mary Ann Glendon, a Professor at Harvard University, wrote an insightful and truly sobering book in 1987 called "Abortion and Divorce in Western Law: American Failures, European Challenges". She argues persuasively that if a country's code of laws is a true barometer of its societal health, then America is in dire straits indeed. This Land has changed, the author affirms, from one of responsible citizenry to one of self-seeking and self-gratification. And she proffers the abortion and divorce laws as probative of her thesis.

Recent news, however, has produced some powerful insights into the abortion quandary. Jody Johnson of Lansdale, PA, a far-out Philadelphia suburb, was all set to adopt Oksana, a six-year-old Russian girl with Down Syndrome, but in late December, 2012, President V. Putin signed a law banning all such adoptions. Jody's heart was broken, as was her purse to the tune of about $50,000. But Jody was not deterred. She is now planning to adopt two brothers, 4 and 6, from another Eastern European country. Her church and neighbors are helping her with the $45,000 adoption and travel fees. Jody hopes and prays to have the boys in the US by the summer of 2015.

Jody Johnson is not alone in seeking adoption. Jim Thompson and his wife Sze Man Yau of Plymouth Meeting, PA, just west of Philadelphia, were fortunate, for they were able to bring home their 2-year old adopted daughter Elena from Russia just three weeks before the Russian ban on adoption. And then there are Ryan and Amber Gager of Atco, NJ. They adopted daughter Lilya from Russia just six months before the December, 2012, ban. Jan Wondra, Acting Chair of Families for Russian and Ukrainian Adoption was quoted in the "Philadelphia Inquirer", January 17, 2014, that at least 1,000 USA families and Slavic children were adversely affected by the Russian ban.

It is clear that tens if not hundreds of thousands of American families are willing to pay any price, travel any distance and suffer any bureaucratic red-tape to adopt a child. Yet, in this country a million plus unborn children are aborted every year! Something surely can be done to remedy this tragedy. Some group surely can step up to the plate. Such a group should have moral clout, serious financial and physical resources and a robust commitment to end abortion in America. The only group on the horizon is the Hierarchy of the Catholic Church.

A national and church-wide program of adoption would be a win-win situation for all parties. The natural mother would gain by carrying her child to term and finding a happy home for it. The adoptive parents would gain by having their fondest dream fulfilled. And the now non-aborted and adopted child would gain life itself! All of America would benefit by not destroying its own littlest ones. The episcopal leaders of such a noble and awe-inspiring movement would gain, once again, the love of the American people, the admiration of their world-wide peers and the truly heavenly acknowledgement of Christ Himself, Who told us all "to let the little children come to me." Pope Francis would be so happy with these Bishops that he might canonize them while they were still alive!

So what we need now is the old-fashioned plan of action (POA). How exactly do we go about convincing pregnant women to forgo abortion, carry a child to term and, if so willing, place it up for adoption?

First we select three major cities in three different geographical areas of the US, such as New York, Chicago and Los Angeles. These urban regions are the locations of three large and resourceful Archdioceses with a good mix of races and religions, poor and rich, and both abortion and adoption seekers. These three centers will be the sites of three pilot projects. We can "baptize" the project with a catchy yet strong name, such as "Give Life, Not Death".

Next we advertise. Billboards in the inner city, fliers in every parish (Catholic, Protestant, Jewish), perhaps radio and TV spots – all this and more ought to do it. The copy should be simple yet direct, something like: ABORTION IS A DEADEND, ADOPTION IS A WAY OUT! IF YOU NEED HELP WITH YOUR PREGNANCY, CALL THIS NUMBER TODAY. HELP IS AS CLOSE AS YOUR CELL. PH No. 000 000 0000. Signed: The Archdiocese of ------------------------.

Thirdly, we staff the Social Service Office of the Archdiocese with a group of compassionate women, lay and sisters, paid and volunteer, to comprise the "Give Life, Not Death" unit. These "Life" workers will have a simple directive. If a pregnant woman is willing to bear and raise her child, we take them to Birthright or a similar society for help. If the woman is willing to bear her child and place it up for adoption, then the staff enrolls her in the "Life" project. The staff then contacts a local Catholic Hospital to make all arrangements for OB-GYN care and a happy delivery. A simple phone call from the Archbishop-Cardinal surely would expedite this care at a "discount" cost to the Archdiocese.

Finally, we put out a call to potential adopting families in the region. Collect their resumes, draw up all the legalities, set a fair price and prepare, we hope, for the brisk business of saving lives and diminishing abortions.

We have no illusions about such a plan. It is not as facile as it may sound and it will not burgeon overnight. Like any new seedling, it will need compassionate care and oversight. But with time and loving labor, it will soon bring forth new life.

Seed money for such a project should be readily available. A few phone calls to New Haven, CT and the Knights of Columbus should do the trick, as well as calls to the many wealthy Catholic business types in abundance around every major city. Besides paying the medical bills of the pregnant woman, such money should be used to provide a modest stipend for the natural mother.

Saving lives is never easy. Moving against the strong tides of selfishness and irresponsibility is never easy. Giving to others is not easy. Yet we are called to do the above by none other the Lord Himself. All we need is a plan!

Just imagine this photo op. Surrounded by beaming nurses and conscientious doctors, the Cardinal Archbishop presents the very first baby of the "Give Life" program to the adoptive parents daubing away at their tears of joy. And then later the 100th child. And soon afterwards the 1,000th child. No words need to be exchanged. This action says it all. The Church is back in business, giving new life to the world, just like Jesus Christ. The Church is back.

And then imagine this scenario. It's September 27, 2015, and Pope Francis is celebrating the closing Mass for the World Meeting of Families in Philadelphia. Some 2 million faithful are gathered on the Benjamin Franklin Parkway to see and pray with the beloved new Pope. And seated in the very front rows, the places of honor, are scores of new parents clutching tenderly their newly adopted infants. The Holy Father whispers a question to the nearest Cardinal-Archbishop at the altar: "Who are these little ones in the front rows?" And the Pope is told that the children are from young mothers who chose to give life rather than abortion and place them in happy homes with good families. Pope Francis beams with joy as he extends his hand in blessing over the children and their new parents, recalling the words of Christ: "Anyone who welcomes this little child in my name welcomes me." (Lk. 9:48)

CHAPTER III

PARISH CLOSURES

One of the most painful experiences for a faithful Catholic is to suffer the closing of his/her local parish. In interviews with parishioners of recently closed parishes, one hears sentiments such as "heartbreaking", "devastating" and "gut-wrenching". The parish was "our spiritual home. Our children were baptized and confirmed in the parish. We attend Mass every Sunday there. The parish was our life, our love. It's like a death in the family."

Parish closures are by no means a localized phenomenon in the USA. Virtually every diocese has closed parishes in the last two decades. Over 1800 parishes have been closed between 1990 and 2010, reports Catholic World News in July of 2011. Over the same time frame the Catholic population in the USA has grown by nearly 50%, from 46 million to over 69 million.

It is clear that such closings, along with parish mergers, are continuing apace into 2014. In the Philadelphia Archdiocese 36 parishes were closed in 2010-2011. In September of 2013 about 40 more parishes were listed as being in danger of closing or merging. Even rural areas are not spared. WLWT

TV in Indianapolis reported in June of 2013 that 27 churches in Southeastern Indiana will be merged or closed within a year. And just about one half of the 130 parishes in the Camden, NJ diocese have been closed or merged in recent years.

Church authorities give a myriad of reasons for parish closings. Among the leading villains in this human drama are the lack of priests, decreased church attendance, decreased financial support by parishioners, demographic shifts and the aging of parish buildings. Certainly, the ongoing scandal of child abuse by Catholic clergy is the proverbial "elephant" in the room. This traumatic tragedy has resulted in the loss of hundreds of clergymen and more than 3 billion dollars in precious assets. Unquantifiable from all these 20 or so years of the scandal are the number of vocations lost, amount of contributions held back by the faithful and the loss of public esteem for the Church.

For the most part parishes are not closed today hastily or haphazardly. Usually a regional cluster of parishes is designated for study as to closing or merging. The Chancery provides certain guidelines for this cluster based on the number of faithful in the area and the availability of priests. Each parish sends a committee of the Pastor and several laity to regular cluster meetings to discuss all the future possibilities. Fact sheets are prepared with the statistical data, such as parish debt and savings, number of baptisms, marriages, deaths, and membership. Meetings go on for months until a consensus is reached on a recommendation, which is sent to the Hierarch. He then makes a decision on which parishes, if any, are to be closed and when.

This process of decision-making seems to be sound and fair to all. However, what is lacking, for the most part, is a follow-up study of how the final decision has worked in real life. Has the decision benefited most if not all the concerned parishioners and priests? For example, how many of the parishioners at a closed parish have registered in the newly designated parish one or two years out. How many have just disappeared? How many have joined another church, perhaps a non-Catholic one? With answers to such questions only then can one judge the wisdom of closing a given parish.

Sociologists, such as James S. Coleman, talk about something called "social capital", the totality of our human relationships built up over the years. This investment of time and money, friendship, love and labor, is located for Catholics in their parish church. Catholics don't go to church for reasons of faith alone. They go to find friends and acceptance, comfort and joy, hope and happiness. So it is only natural that Catholics feel such anger and pain of heart when their parish is closed. This is why the faithful in Detroit protested and occupied their parish church when Cardinal Szoka closed 43 parishes a few decades ago. And this is why the faithful in Cleveland protested and appealed to the Vatican (and won!) when their churches were closed.

One aspect of parish-closure process rarely mentioned by the decision makers is the final disposition of the parish property. In other words, what's to become of the church building, rectory, hall, school, convent and land itself? Are there clear plans in place for these now unused assets? Or will they be allowed to stand empty for years and slowly disintegrate? To have to drive by one's former parish estate and see it rotting in place by disuse would only rekindle the hurt and anger of its closure.

Certainly, there are some real and convincing reasons for closing down a parish. Money, or rather the lack thereof is right on top of the list. If a parish cannot pay its bills and chronically must beg or borrow from the Chancery, it should be placed on fiscal probation for a year. Once the Pastor and parishioners are so informed and still cannot make ends meet, then closure is clearly in order.

Another obvious indicator for closure of a parish is weak and falling membership. If a Pastor and the Faithful do not attract new members and the death rate far exceeds the baptism numbers, this should be a red flag for all concerned. There is a tipping point in every parish below which it becomes difficult if not impossible to sustain a healthy institution. Morale diminishes, social life lessons, fund-raising falters, spiritual life wanes and a slow death spiral ensues. Again, a year or so of probation is called for and, if things do not improve, eventual closure is indicated.

In these two instances it is really the parish itself, both Pastor and Faithful that are the deciders. The parish is being shuttered because of its inability to support itself or gain new members. The bishop is simply executing the natural law of survival. No commonsensical man or woman can fault the Bishop for the decision of closure of a parish that is slowly dying of its own accord.

The main reason for closing a parish, Church authorities indicate, is the lack of priests. This thinking seems to make sense, for in the experience of most Catholics it is the Priest-Pastor who heads the Parish, leads the prayers, performs services, conducts the meetings and signs the checks. No priest – no parish! Perfectly understandable! But maybe there's a way or two to cut this Gordian Knot to save viable parishes from closing? And we are not talking about ordaining women or married men here, subjects beyond the modest purview of this essay. To this point we offer two simple proposals.

The first is to "ask" the younger priests to do double duty in order to save a neighboring parish from closing. Allow the priest to take a double salary so that he can hire a driver and, perhaps, an order priest from the neighboring Catholic college for the holydays. Staff both parishes with capable janitorial and secretarial workers. Assign the priest for a limited term, say three years or so with a proviso for an extension. And give the priest an extra week of summer vacation. And it should all work out.

A priest friend served as Pastor for two churches for 16 years. The parishes were ten miles apart over hilly roads, but Father was rarely late for the six or seven weekend services in both parishes. He travelled with a driver and cantor and organized the laity to perform all the typical pastoral tasks, such as banking, printing, record-keeping, fund-raising and social directing. Father watched his health, rested his body and soul Monday and Tuesday. By the next weekend he was ready to go back to working a double shift. Both parishes thrived during Father's tenure and are alive and well in 2014.

There is no thought here that such an arrangement is easily done. It takes a strong priest and an understanding flock. But it's being done throughout this country, especially within the Eastern-rite Catholic and Orthodox Churches. It is not the ideal situation for all parishes would like to have their own resident Pastor. But it certainly beats closing a parish. And if a given parish is willing to share their priest with another flock, the Bishop should be willing to make it happen.

The other reasonable alternative to closing a parish is commonly referred to as a "priestless parish'". Simply put, in this situation the laity administer the parish and arrange for a priest or deacon to have all the necessary services. It may surprise some to learn that as of 2013 there were 49,172 priestless parishes in the world, reports the Center for Applies Research at Georgetown U. CARA Services also reports that as of 2010 there were 3,342 priestless parishes in the USA. And this phenomenon is growing rapidly.

It is revealing and certainly comforting, especially to all the legalists among us, that the new Code of Canon Law of the Roman Church provides for such priestless parishes. Canon 517, par. 2 reads: "If, because of the shortage of priests, the diocesan bishop has judged that a deacon, or some other person who is not a priest or a community of persons, should be entrusted with a share in the exercise of the pastoral care of a parish, he is to appoint some priest who with the powers and faculties of a parish priest, will direct the pastoral care." The canon is clear that, while a priest is to ultimately oversee the spiritual care of a parish, the laity can be appointed to administer the daily parish operations.

Bishops around the world have found creative ways to keep their parishes open without a permanent and resident priest-pastor. Rocco Palmo reported ("Whispers in the Loggia", 2008) that Bishop Kettler of Alaska's Fairbanks Diocese has only 17 priests with 47 parishes. The Bishop and eight urban priests leave the cities and fly out to the bush to tend to the far-flung flock, while deacons and lay presiders provide services back home in the cities. The event was called "Priestless Sunday" for the Catholic urban dwellers.

Bishop Tony Taylor of Little Rock, AR, spoke about his experience in Kenya during his diaconal year of training, reported R. Palmo (Ibid.). The young deacon served in a parish with 40,000 Catholics and just two priests. Four church buildings and 28 chapels comprised the parish. Some 12 trained lay catechists conducted services at all the sites when the priests were celebrating Mass elsewhere. Astoundingly, at least 85% of the faithful attended worship services every week.

In Wendell, Idaho, Sister Mary Louise Deroin, a Holy Cross nun, is a Pastoral Administrator of St. Anthony Parish and St. Catherine Parish, 12 miles apart. She regularly celebrates a Communion service when a priest is not available, reported the "Los Angeles Times" in1989. About 36 of the 110 parishes in the Boise Diocese were without resident priests.

The Institute of Pastoral Life in Kansas City, MO, has trained hundreds of lay men and women to become Pastoral Administrators, who will serve to keep parishes open in the absence of a resident priest. This Church-supported institute suggests some 85% of all USA dioceses will soon have priestless parishes that will be kept open by lay administrators, reports the same "LA Times" article.

Lay Ministry is a very hot topic in the Catholic Church today. In fact, the Committee on the Laity is a subordinate group within the Conference of Catholic Bishops and is overseen by eight hierarchs in the US. Lay formation programs now operate in more than 65% of US dioceses with more than 300 training programs with a total enrollment of 35,000 in 2001, reports the "Call to the Laity" by Helen Keeler and Susan Grimbly. The women write: "Because there are not enough priests to fulfill all the diocesan duties… lay Catholics accept the roles of formation director, parish life coordinator, and pastoral associates…to take on some of the responsibilities normally carried out by priests in diocesan offices, parishes and seminaries all over the United States".

Here's the situation right now. It's the last quarter of the Big Game out on the hardwood. The starters on the home team are beginning to falter. They're well-worn and tired. The rookies on the bench are fired-up, willing and able to go in. The game is on the line. The Coach must make a DECISION: Likely lose with the starters or win with the bench. Timeout is called. The Ref waits for a decision The Coach must decide. It's now or never.

CHAPTER IV

THE CLERGY SEX ABUSE SCANDAL

During the past 1,000 years there have been several epochal tragedies in the history of the Catholic Church. In the 11th century the Church became estranged and finally separated from the Eastern Orthodox Church. In the 11th to 13th centuries the Church conducted seven Crusades that ultimately resulted in the death of millions and the devastation of cities and relations between East and West. From the 15th to the 17th centuries the Spanish Inquisition brought about torture and death to untold thousands and lasting ill will for the Church. And then there was the Protestant Reformation of the 16th century which permanently splintered Western Christendom. In the last half of the 20th century still another tragedy has befallen the Church, the clergy sex abuse crisis. While hindsight is readily available to study the long-term effects of these earlier tragedies, the abuse scandal continues to play out today and its historic consequences cannot be accurately judged. However, one can analyze the current depth of this crisis and suggest some helpful remedial actions for the Church.

The main victims in this scandal are the teen and pre-teen survivors of sexual abuse on the part of clergymen: bishops, priests, deacons and seminarians. In 2002 the US Conference of Catholic Bishops commissioned the John Jay College of Criminal Justice (CUNY) to assemble an exhaustive report on this scandal. The report was to include both a qualitative and quantitative analysis. This report appeared in February of 2004 and documented 10,667 cases of abuse of minors by clerics between 1950 and 2002.

The number of abused victims has apparently increased dramatically since 2002. As of May 9, 2013, the USCCB reported 16, 795 cases of child abuse by clerics from 1950 to 2012. This figure was compiled by BishopAccountability. org in 2013 from the USCCB data. In 2012 alone there were 471 cases of credible charges of sexual abuse of minors by clerics in the USA Church. Certainly, the primary victims of this scandal were the abused children. But their families also suffered great pain and long-term suffering. When one considers the parents, siblings, relatives, friends and neighbors of the survivors, only then can one judge the extent of this crisis. This multiplier effect indicates that hundreds of thousands of victims have been harmed and hurt by the sexual abuse scandal in the US Church.

A subset of victims of the abuse scandal is the large number of good and faithful clerics who are the recipients of scorn and profanity in their daily rounds. Many have changed their ministerial activities to a more reclusive lifestyle to avoid all contact with parish youth. They have been forced to face grilling and angry questions from the faithful, who clearly distrust their pastors and school chaplains. About 110,000 priests have served the US Church from 1950 to 2002 and about 5.5% have been charged with the crime of abuse of minors.

But the 94.5% of innocent clerics have paid a heavy price for the crimes of their colleagues.

Another victim of the abuse scandal is the Church itself. Its credibility has been shaken, its ministers demoralized, its faithful angered. In many parishes collections are down and pews are less full. Traditional enemies of the Church now have new ammunition to fire their guns of scorn and hate. Pastors and school principals are now burdened with collecting reams of files to prove the good character of all their CCD, elementary and high school staff. With the bishops, priests and laity there now is a clear and palpable sense of anger and confusion. The entire Church is suffering.

It is disheartening for people of good will to see that the wounds of this abuse scandal upon the Church are entirely self-inflicted. There was some early talk by Church authorities that the media were blameworthy for "making a mountain out of a molehill." And then there were the other usual suspects, such as humanism, secularism and modernism. But as the scandal began to unravel it became clear to all that the causative agents were two: failure of Church leadership and pedophiliac clergy.

In the last 62 years (1950 – 2012) at least 6, 275 clerics were credibly accused of sexual abuse of minors in the US Church, reports BishopAccountability.org on May 9, 2013. This figure is on the low side because no data were available for the year 2003. About 56% of the names of these accused clerics have been revealed, 3,818 individuals, in a database maintained by BishopAccountability.org.

Full information has been released on 3,492 accused clerics, which includes 3,397 priests, 23 bishops, 52 deacons and 20 seminarians. The most recent data indicate that in 2011 some 167 priests were credibly accused of child abuse in the US. In 2012 that number remained about the same with 160 Catholic priests "not implausibly" charged with abuse of minors.

In the 2004 report by the John Jay Institute on Criminal Justice on sexual abuse within the Church a profile was provided on the accused perpetrators. It was revealed that most of the charged priests were ordained between 1950 and 1979 (68%). The largest group of accused priests, over 40%, were in their thirties when abuse occurred. Some 42.3% of the priests were associate pastors at the time of abuse. The majority of priests, 56%, were charged with abusing one victim. Many of these clerics (32%) were discovered to have had other behavioral or psychological problems. (John Jay Report, pp. 5-6).

Beginning in 1985 with the guilty plea of Fr. Gilbert Gauthe in Louisiana to eleven counts of abusing minors, the criminal cases and lawsuits began in court. As of 2012 more than 3,000 civil lawsuits have been filed against the Church and its clerics, reported Michael D. Schaffer. The Associated Press estimated in 2007 that the total monetary settlements from 1950 to 2007 abuse cases reached more 2 billion dollars. This figure increased to more than 3 billion by 2012, reported Bishop Accountability. Between 2004 and 2011 eight Roman Catholic dioceses declared bankruptcy as a result of abuse case settlements.

The court-awarded settlements were not the only financial loss to the Church. Anger over the abuse scandal prompted the faithful in the pews, in some instances, to reduce or even withhold their weekly donations. The removal from ministry of hundreds of accused clerics cost the Church in sorely needed manpower. The expense of commissioning studies and extraordinary meetings was in the millions. The moral cost of the loss of trust and credibility remains incalculable. This mistrust was regularly strengthened by the negative publicity in the mass media over new cases of clergy abusing minors. Even the United Nations felt compelled to report out on the Church's scandal. On February 6, 2013, The Philadelphia Inquirer reported on page one that the UN "demanded that the Vatican immediately turn over to criminal investigators any known or suspected abusers and end its 'code of silence' by enforcing rules ordering dioceses to report abuse to local authorities."

The rising tide of the abuse scandal was nearing full flood by 2002 with some 4,392 clergymen named as abusers since 1950. The US bishops had to act. They met in Dallas, TX, in June of 2002 and approved The Charter for the Protection of Children and Young People. This document was revised twice, in June of 2005, and in June of 2011. The bishops thereby mandated a "zero tolerance policy" for clerical abusers, safe environment policies for all parishes and schools, the reporting of all abuse cases to the proper local authorities and transparency toward the public in regard to these matters. One of the fruits of the Charter was the promulgation on May 6, 2006, of 13 "Essential Norms" as particular laws for all US dioceses. These norms mandate the creation of a Review Board in every diocese to study every case of sex abuse and advise the bishop accordingly. Also mandated by the Norms is the temporary removal from ministry of a suspected sexual abuser, as well as the permanent removal if guilt is determined. Norm No. 11 obliges the dioceses to comply with all civil laws in regard to the reporting of alleged crimes. The final Norm regards the need to protect the rights of all parties, especially the accuser and the clerical suspect, in the instance of child abuse.

Another fruitful result of the Dallas meeting was the appointment of a National Review Board composed of prominent lay members. The Board was tasked in 2002 with determining the facts and figures of the abuse scandal in the Church. Board members promptly commissioned the John Jay College of Criminal Justice in New York to provide a comprehensive report on the nature and scope of the scandal, which was completed and published in 2004. This study was augmented in 2010 with a report on the causes and context of the scandal.

The John Jay Report identified several factors contributing to the abuse scandal, according to B. A. Robinson: failure of the bishops to grasp the seriousness of the problem, overemphasis on trying to avoid scandal, use of unqualified treatment centers, misguided willingness to forgive and insufficient accountability. To keep current with the regular flow of data on the abuse scandal, the US Bishops commissioned the Center for Applied Research in the Apostolate of Georgetown University, Washington, DC. Besides providing annual figures on both the accused clerics and the victims since the spring of 2005, the Center also is charged with auditing individual dioceses as to their implementation of the Dallas Charter and Essential Norms. The latest report released by the Center was that of May 9, 2013, which showed that there were 160 clerics accused of sexual abuse and 471 survivor-victims in 2012.

Charters were drafted, laws were promulgated, norms were established, data were collected and analyzed, review boards were formed, statistics were documented and apologies were printed. What else can the bishops do to remedy the fallout of the clergy sex scandal, which they themselves call "a crisis without precedent in our times" in their Preamble to the 2011 document to the Dallas Charter and its Revisions?

The first and main thing the bishops can and should do is reach out to the American people and convey to them, in summary, the whole story of the abuse scandal in the USA. The American people may know bits and pieces from the daily newspapers or 20-second blurbs on TV, but they simply deserve to hear the entire history of this experience. They deserve to hear the extent of the moral and legal failures of the clergymen, the number of victims and all the remedies put in place by the bishops. Until this is done the scandal will continue to fester in the minds and hearts of the men and women in the pews and streets of the US.

How can this be done? In today's world there is only one way – on prime time television. The hierarchs can purchase a half hour of TV time Sunday and select a qualified and non-controversial member of their corps to address the American People. Dressed in a black suit and pectoral cross, this bishop should open and close the segment with an apology from all the bishops to all Americans, especially to all the victim-survivors. He can give the latest number of abusive clerics, as well as victims, and then describe all the many remedies the bishops have taken to date to deal with this scandal. Finally, the speaker should ask the viewers for their forgiveness and prayers.

The American People, especially the Catholics, desperately want to hear from these spiritual leaders. Unless and until they so hear, the drumbeat of distrust and anger will go on tomorrow and beyond. There is another group of "secondary victims" in the abuse crisis that should be addressed. This is the band of brothers to the bishop, the 95 percenters, the good and faithful priests of the diocese. These men are tired and demoralized by the scandal. They have many questions but few answers. They worry about their own fate, civil and canonical rights, if they are ever (falsely) accused. They are even the object of scornful questions and angry looks on the street. These faithful servants deserve to hear from their bishop. Every diocesan bishop should gather his faithful priests, in a display of the transparency promised by the Dallas Charter, and speak to them from his brotherly heart. First the bishop should thank all the men for their faithfulness to the Gospel of Jesus Christ. It would not hurt to also thank all the pastors for their continuing financial support to cover all the expenses precipitated by the abuse scandal which funds also provide for the normal operation of the bishop's staff and office. Then the hierarch can give all the facts and figures on the accused clerics and surviving victims. A question and answer session might conclude the meeting.

You can be sure that such a gathering of brothers around their candid and respectful bishop would go a long way in healing the pain of the good and faithful servants of the Lord.

For several decades now the Catholic Church in the US has struggled through a great crisis, the clergy abuse scandal. The suffering was deep and widespread. Anger and confusion still haunt the pews, living-rooms and streets of this land. These wounds of so many are much too fresh for a full closure today. But at least some temporary respite and clarity are now possible, if the bishops would step up and address these issues with the American People and their brother priests. It's time for some good old-fashioned candor and transparency. The American People and the faithful priests deserve to be enlightened about all these recent events in their Church.

CHAPTER V

CONTRACEPTION

Hiding in plain sight, like the proverbial elephant in the room, is the moral issue of contraception or birth control among the array of problems for the Catholic Church today. It is not primarily a contentious issue in the USA because most Catholics, female and male, ignore its condemnation by the Church. And precisely therein lies the rub.

The Church has a clear and long-standing record of condemning contraception. Virtually all Catholics are aware of this ban. Yet most Catholics, married and single, young and old, male and female continue to ignore this ban and practice various forms of birth control. This ethical schism results in a serious distrust for Catholics in the moral Magisterium or teaching authority of the Church. On the other hand, the Church authorities, the bishops surely must sense unease and frustration over the failure of their teaching, which is being mostly ignored.

This moral impasse needs to be addressed for the sake of both the bishops of the Church and the laity. On the one hand, the credibility of the Church's teaching authority is at stake. On the other hand, the peace of conscience of the laity in their daily life of intimate love is at risk.

Let's first look at the teaching of the Church on contraception. In the Hebrew Scripture (Old Testament) the story of Onan (Gen. 38) had been cited in the past as evidence of the evil of contraception. But virtually all modern scriptural scholars agree that the Lord took Onan's life not because he spilled his seed on the ground, but because he refused to father a child with his late brother's widow, as mandated in the Mosaic law (Deut. 35:5-6). It is clear that Onan's sin was not that of contraception, but that of dishonoring his family, that of his father Judah.

In the New Testament there are two passages that seem to condemn contraception. These two sources (Ga. 5:20 and Rev. 21:8, 22:15) list a host of sins, including the Greek terms "mageia" and "pharmakeia". John A. Hardon, S.J. in his "The Catholic Catechism", 1975, regards these passages as an implicit condemnation of contraception, as he translates the two words as "magic" and "drugs". However, Biblical scholars such as the translators of the Jerusalem Bible, New American Bible, the Chicago Bible and even the old Douay-Rheims version use the words "idolatry" and "sorcery" to denote these two evils. These Biblicists obviously see no direct reference to contraception in Galatians or Revelation.

To sum up the Biblical evidence in regard to the morality of contraception, there is no direct or unambiguous condemnation of this practice. John T. Noonan Jr. wrote the most exhaustive and definitive work on contraception in memory. First published in 1965 by Harvard University Press, Cambridge, MA, the work was titled "Contraception: A History of Its Treatment by the Catholic Theologians and Canonists" and was revised in 1986. In regard to the sin of Onan, Noonan writes on p. 35: "That contraception as such was condemned seems unlikely. There is no commandment against contraception in any of the codes of law." Commenting on the New Testament texts of Galatians and Revelation, Noonan concludes: "One cannot tell from the condemnations of 'pharmakeia' presented in the New Testament whether only certain of the drugs used for evil purposes were condemned, or whether a contraception potion fell within the category of bad medicine." (p. 45)

The Apostolic Fathers were a group of early Christian writers, who witnessed to various Church teachings and liturgical rites during the second century of the new Faith. There are, however, several strong passages of moral exhortations, especially in the Didache and Epistle of Barnabas. The Kirsopp Lake translation, reprinted in 1970 by the Harvard University Press, has the Didachist condemning in Ch. V: "adulteries, lusts, fornications, thefts, idolatries, witchcrafts, charms. . ." The Epistle of Barnabas has a similar sin-list of condemned practices in Ch. XX, including "enchantments and magic". While some modern authors interpret these practices as contraceptive in nature, it is difficult to be certain about the real intentions of these two early Christian authors. The two Greek words for sins in the texts ("mageia, pharmakeia") simply can be understood in different ways.

As the threat of the Gnostic heresies increased in the third century, this amalgam of pagan philosophy, magical rituals and sexual aberrations prompted Christian writers to clarify the orthodox moral teaching of the Church on sexuality. Among the earliest condemnations of contraception were those of Clement of Alexandria in "Paedagogus", Marcus Minucius Felix in his "Octavius" and in the "Elenchus" attributed widely to Hippolytus. Writing in c. 300 a.d., Lactantius ("The Divine Institutes") condemns various sexual practices which have a contraceptive effect. The Stoic teaching that procreation is the natural and ethical purpose of sexual intercourse seems to have played no small role in the thinking of these Christian authors, as they defended the developing moral code of the Church against the Gnostics.

Of all the Church Fathers the most influential moral teacher is St. Augustine (354-430), the Bishop of Hippo. In matters of marriage, sexuality and sin this North African wandered through the theological thickets of Manicheanism, Platoism and finally Christianity, when he was baptized by St. Ambrose of Milan on Easter Eve, 387. Augustine's teaching on marriage is set forth in two works of 388: "The Morals of the Manichees" and "The Morals of the Catholic Church". The Saint taught that the sole purpose of marriage and the marital act is procreation. Any sexual activity between spouses that vitiates this purpose is sinful, Augustine wrote. It is interesting that this Church Father condemns even intercourse during the sterile period as contraceptive and therefore sinful, when Catholic theologians and authorities today regard this "rhythm method" as morally acceptable. Revolted by the Manichean opposition to all procreation and inspired by the natural law teaching of Stoicism, Augustine vigorously presents the case to condemn all forms of contraception in marriage. The Catholic Church and most Protestant Churches followed his lead for centuries.

The early Church Fathers were star-struck by the powerful light of Plato's idealistic philosophy, but this Greek's star began to fade with the medieval discovery of his student Aristotle's brilliance. Exemplifying best this turn to the empiricism of Aristotle's philosophy was St. Thomas Aquinas (1225-1275), the Church's superstar of scholastic theology and philosophy. This Italian-born Dominican developed his theory of natural law in his "Summa Theologica", "Summa contra Gentiles" and "On the Sentences". Thomas held that the end purpose of marital coitus, according to the natural law, is the generation of the species. Therefore, any action taken to subvert this end is contraceptive and sinful, i.e. against nature. This view of the evil of contraceptive practices held sway in the Church for centuries. In fact, Pope Paul VI in his encyclical "Humanae Vitae" (1968) condemned contraception partly on the basis that it transgressed against "Natural Law".

The tone for the Church's moral teaching in the modern era was set in the papacy of Pius IX (1846-1878) and his "Syllabus of Errors", along with its explanatory Encyclical "Quanta Cura" of 1864. These works condemned moral relativism, science, even freedom of speech and democracy, establishing the Church as the sole beacon of truth and moral teaching in the world. The decree of Vatican I on papal infallibility in 1879 sealed the deal on the Church's authority to pronounce on faith and morals, including, of course, contraception.

By the late 1920's the practice of contraception was growing in Europe and the Americas, such that Roman Catholic authorities were becoming alarmed. When the Anglican Church at the Lambeth Conference in August of 1930 voted that birth control was morally acceptable, it shook and shocked Pope Pius XI into action. He produced the encyclical "Casti connubii" and promulgated it December 31, 1930, as the definitive teaching on marriage. Citing at length sources from Scripture, Church Fathers, medieval theologians and papal predecessors, Pius XI provided his flock with the most comprehensive teaching to date on the nature of marriage, along with a condemnation of contraception.

The turbulent times of the 1960's signaled to many that dramatic changes were afoot in the world. The Church was no exception with Vatican II, the first Ecumenical Council in 95 years, and the papacies of two exceptional men, John XXIII and Paul VI. Priests were convinced that optional celibacy was on the near horizon, as were the laity in regard to lifting the ban on contraception. Both were sorely disappointed. Pope Paul VI reaffirmed the discipline of priestly celibacy with his June 12,

1967, encyclical "Sacerdotalis Caelibatus". The same Pope reiterated the Church's strong condemnation of contraception in the summer of 1968 with his encyclical "Humanae Vitae".

Although "Humanae Vitae" clearly opposed contraceptive practices, it did include "conjugal love" among spouses as a purpose for marital intercourse along with the ever-present end of procreation. Commenting on the Encyclical just a few days after publication, Pope Paul VI indicated that the letter was not a complete work on marriage and that the Magisterium should and could return to this subject in the future.

Pope John Paul II did return to the matter of morality in marriage with his 1981 Apostolic Exhortation "Familiaris Consortio". Although artificial contraceptive acts were clearly condemned by Papa Wojtyla, he did give much credence to the notion that the marriage act was one of love between spouses. This unitive purpose of marriage became conjoined with its procreative purpose as the standard Catholic theology since the 1980's. And this is where things stand today, half-way through the second decade of the 21st century, in the official teaching of the Church: there are two main purposes in marriage, the procreative and the unitive; all contraceptive practices are banned, with the exception of the rhythm method.

This is exactly where the problem lies for the Church. The laity, by a large majority accept gladly the first proposition on purposes, but reject strongly the second proposition on contraception. There is some current (2014) debate about the exact number of Catholic women who use contraception. The "Think Progress" website of September 19, 2013, asserts that 82% of Catholics think that birth control is morally acceptable, while the Guttmacher Report of April 2011, shows that 98% of Catholic women have used contraceptives. Whereas the exact number may be in doubt, one matter is not in doubt: the Catholic laity and Church authorities clearly disagree on contraception. In order to restore moral harmony in the Church, either the Bishops (including the Bishop of Rome) or the Faithful will have to change.

It is highly unlikely that the faithful will change their mind on contraception. Modern man and woman, especially the latter as the final judge and decider on the number and spacing of children in the family, are challenged today by powerful forces in society. These social, economic, demographic and personal forces strongly mitigate against large families today. The only reasonable option is for the Church authorities to somehow moderate their teaching on birth control.

In the recent past the Church has changed its moral teaching on many issues, such as usury, slavery, the Friday fast and women's rights. Perhaps the most striking example of alterations in the Church's moral doctrine is its about-face in regard the 1864 "Syllabus of Errors" of Pius IX. This Pontiff condemned such things as progress, democracy, liberalism, modernism and scientism among others in his list of "errors". Today's church quietly ignores such 19th century teaching, realizing that these condemned phenomena were both time and condition specific.

So one approach open to the Church in regard birth control, freely and wisely chosen by caring spouses, is a purposeful silence. If such spouses act in good conscience for the benefit of their family, they would not be condemned for their contraceptive practice. The Church would simple trust faithful Catholic spouses to do what is necessary for the good of their family. This approach is similar to that taken by the Church in regard the "Syllabus of Errors".

Another possible approach would be to lessen the gravity of the moral ban on contraception. From one of a grievous or mortal sin to one of failing to practice the ideal Catholic teaching on birth control might be a plausible position for today's Church. One can see such a moral position in the matter of usury, the formerly sinful practice of charging interest, in the thinking of today's Church. Taking of any interest on a loan was strongly condemned by the Medieval Church. Today a modest interest rate on a loan is morally acceptable, witness the Vatican Bank.

A third avenue toward a solution would be for the Church to recognize and accept certain exceptions to the ban on birth control. Such exemptions might be the health of the wife, financial constraints, welfare of existing children in the family, age of husband or wife, medical advice and warning. Consider the Fifth Commandment, "Thou shall not kill", perhaps the strictest prohibition in all the Mosaic Law in regard to a neighbor. Yet, there are clear exceptions to this law embraced by the Church, such as self-defense, just war, even capital punishment in prior years. There are very few moral absolutes in moral theology. Contraception is most probably not among them.

The main and sole purpose of this work is to alleviate the anguish of conscience for Catholics practicing birth control, as well as restore the credibility of the Church. The Bishop of Rome, Pope Francis seems to share this concern. In a lengthy interview conducted right after his election, in March of 2013, the Pontiff said that "the Church has grown too obsessed with moral issues like abortion, birth control and gay marriages". The Holy Father concludes the Italian-outlet interview by saying that "the dogmatic and moral teachings of the Church are not all equivalent." It only remains for the episcopal brothers of the Bishop of Rome to work out a modern solution to the age-old problem of contraception for their faithful flocks.

Chapter VI

Vocations

Long before the AccuWeather meteorological service was formed at Penn State in 1962 to predict the weather for the local dairy farmers in Central Pennsylvania, people used the old pressure-sensitive liquid barometer to foretell the incoming weather. Without this trusty device there was no accurate way to know and plan for tomorrow's weather. The Church has such a barometer of sorts that can provide its bishops with a clear picture of its future health. Vocations to the priesthood constitute this barometer.

The 1960's were the high-water mark for the number of seminarians enrolled in the USA. The academic year of 1967-1968 boasted a virtual flood of some 8,000 theologians and 13,400 college seminary students. About 16,000 students were registered in seminary prep schools. The Center for Applied Research in the Apostolate (CARA), Georgetown University, reported on April, 2013, that the average retention rate for theologians from year one to ordination was about 75%. In those halcyon days the Church could look forward to some 1500 priestly ordinations every spring, a figure that includes both diocesan and religious priests. These new ordinands joined their older cohorts in the priesthood, some 56,000 strong, to serve about 47 million US Catholics in the middle 1960's.

As the US Catholic population grew steadily in the 1970's and 1980's by about 5 million per decade, the seminaries, in contrast, began to empty out. Reasons given for this phenomenon are many and varied, such as disappointment over Vatican II and Papal teachings, societal turmoil, smaller family size, priests leaving their celibate calling and new generational values. By the 1988-89 academic year only 3,788 students were counted in US seminaries, reported CARA. The number of major seminarians, in theology and philosophy, leveled out during the 1994-2009 period to about 5,000 students per annum. This figure breaks down to about 3,500 diocesan and 1,500 religious seminarians throughout these 15 years.

In more recent times the "Catholic Almanac" published by Our Sunday's Visitor in 2012, lists 5,247 seminarians for 2011, with a breakdown of 3,394 for the USA dioceses and 1,853 for the religious orders. It is noteworthy that preparatory or high school seminaries have all but disappeared from the US scene. Only four such schools remained open in 2011 with a total of 448 students.

The ordination class of 2013 included 497 men, according to CARA. This figure represented 129 new religious order priests and 369 diocesan priests to join in serving some 70 million US Catholics. The bottom line here is that, compared to the 1960's the ordination rate of new priests has fallen today some 65%, while the number of Catholics has increased 50%. At best, these facts and figures should be sobering if not deeply troubling for all the bishops of the US Church.

The first casualty of the priest shortage is the closing of parishes. Over 1800 parishes have been closed in the

1990-2010 timeframe. Several hundred more have been shuttered in the last three years. These figures tally a full 12% of the 18,000 parishes listed in the "Catholic Almanac" for 2012. When a given parish is closed or merged, all the parishioners do not march in lockstep to join the newly designated parish. In fact, many simply drop out and leave the Church. Anecdotal evidence puts the number of "lost souls" at about 40-45%, meaning that tens if not hundreds of thousands of Catholics are being lost to the Church on a regular basis as more parishes are closed or merged.

Another clear casualty of the decline in vocations is the morale of the priests. The average age of a US Catholic priest today is about 58, an age when many professional men are preparing to retire. Yet the typical parish priest is being told to take on more work, as parishes are being closed and new recruits are fewer in number and older in age. The Philadelphia Archdiocese is using today the metric of 5,000 faithful per priest as the guideline for placement of clergy. The result is more work, less parishes and low morale for a given priest-pastor. The consequences of such a situation are fairly obvious. The priests will suffer, as ultimately will also the faithful and the Church itself.

The shortage of priests-pastors today results in a loss of millions of dollars to the Church at large. In a typical priest's professional lifetime he oversees the production of many millions of dollars for various causes, such as the maintenance of the parish, the foreign missions, the Vatican, the poor and hungry, as well as the local economy. In addition, every parish sends a significant monthly stipend to the bishop's Chancery. Usually amounting to about 12% of a parish's annual income, the loss of this stipend to the Chancery due to closed parishes and lack of priests translates into millions of dollars of lost revenue for the Church.

There is a bit of a vicious circle operative now as regards the recruitment of vocations to the priesthood. The main promoter of vocations has always been the parish priest. With low morale and low numbers today's pastors are by and large not performing this task. And as vocations shrink and new priests dwindle in number, the morale of their older cohorts continues to sink.

Another powerful force in promoting vocations to the priesthood is the family circle, especially the mother. But both mothers and fathers are hesitant today in encouraging their sons to enter the seminary for a variety of reasons. The size of the nuclear family in the USA is diminishing significantly from past generations with the exception of the Hispanic and African-American populations. So there are less young men to send off to the seminary and a celibate life. Also, parents are well aware of the legal and moral failings, even trials and incarceration, of so many clergymen that even good Catholic faithful look askance at such a vocation for their sons.

But all is not lost, one might think, for there is a third source for producing vocations apart from the Parish Priest and the family. This tried and true vocation-grower is the local parochial school. For many decades now the good sisters have hammered home the idea of the seminary to the impression-able minds of the 8th- grade boys. And it worked! Vocations were off the charts until the 1970's, but then the sisters began to disappear from the classrooms and the schools themselves began to close. Between 2000 and 2010, reports the NCEA, the number of Catholic elementary and secondary schools fell from 8,146 to 6,980, a drop of 117 per year. In addition, the number of religious sisters staffing the schools fell from 179, 954 in 1965 to 57,544 in 2010. Today only 2.6% of Catholic teachers are nuns, writes "The Catholic World Report" in

May, 2011. Translation: fewer schools and fewer sisters equal fewer vocations.

If priests are not promoting, schools not producing and sisters not around to foster vocations to the priesthood, what's to be done by the bishops of the USA Church? One solution trumpeted often by both priests and laity is to make celibacy optional for the priesthood, as it is in the Eastern Churches, both Catholic and Orthodox. As recently as May 2014, an op-ed piece by Paul V. Kane, a former fellow at Harvard's Kennedy School, called for the formation of a papal commission to study the celibacy requirement with a view toward abolishing this law. The fact that there are 50,000 parishes worldwide without a resident priest calls for such a dramatic change in clerical discipline, concludes Kane in the "Philadelphia Daily News", May 5, 2014. Both individually and in their associations, priests have spoken loud and clear about the need for optional celibacy in the Church. Even a handful of Bishops has weighed in to support a change in the celibacy rule. While the view of Pope Francis on this subject cannot be definitely known today, at least he seems to be open to discussion on the matter.

Of course, there are many voices within the Church opposed to changing the mandatory celibacy discipline for priests. Perhaps the most outspoken and popular writer on the subject in this generation was the late Chicago priest Father Andrew M. Greeley. While he was in favor of the ordination of women to the priesthood, he opposed altering the celibacy role for priests. Father Greeley opined that the transcendental or heavenly character of the celibate priesthood, so attractive to the laity in today's worldly society, would be lost if priests were married. ("The Catholic Myth", Charles Scribner's Sons, 1990, pp. 147-148).

While the long-term outcome of this debate and even resolution cannot be fathomed today, the immediate future is clear. Celibacy will be in effect this year and the next, as the vocation shortage continues to cripple the Church.

Back in the 1950's and 1960's it was commonplace to hear a foreign accent in the confessional and from the pulpit in Catholic churches. These predominantly Irish and Polish priests fled post-war Europe to fill the gaps to teach in the burgeoning Catholic Schools and preach in hundreds of new churches built to accommodate the booming post-war population in the USA. But things are different today. With exception of Poland and Western Ukraine, the Catholic dioceses of Europe can hardly fill their own clerical needs and are in no position to assist their USA counterparts.

Some African countries like Nigeria seem to have an excess of priests, who might be of assistance in filling the vocation gap in the USA. But such thinking is deceptive. The Catholic population of Africa was given in 2011 as 180 million with about 37,000 priests, as listed in the "Catholic Almanac", 2012. These figures indicate that the ratio of priests to faithful in Africa is similar to that in the USA. For the US Bishops to import clergy from Africa would amount to one of the better examples of the phrase "robbing Peter to pay Paul".

It is a truism that a healthy and mature church must have native-born clergy. The importation of priests is only a stop-gap measure, historically used for missionary purposes. The bishops all know this. They must somehow increase vocations among their own flocks or suffer quite negative consequences.

There are several extraordinary measures the Church might take to increase vocations. Leading the list is the ordination of women. There is no doubt that thousands of US women are willing and quite capable of becoming priests. Recent

Popes and most bishops, however, are unwilling to consider this possibility. Pope John Paul II in his 1994 Apostolic Letter "Sacerdotalis Ordinatio" banned even the consideration of women priests. The Pontiff writes: "I declare that the Church has no authority whatsoever to confer priestly ordination on women, and that this judgment is to be definitely held by all the Church's faithful."

Another possible step to promote vocations would be the implementation of term limits on the priesthood, whereby the newly ordained priest would serve a period of 20 years, for example, and then decide to continue or embark on another career. This idea is patterned after the US armed forces and was introduced by scholars like Andrew M. Greeley in the 1990's. The problem here is that the Church has a long-standing history of declaring the priesthood as "eternal". Once a priest, always a priest, the saying goes. The high irony here is that even the Pope cannot "unmake" Father X, who is serving 30 years in prison for abusing 20 children. The ordination ritual states: "you are a priest forever according to the order of Melchisedek."

A third possible route for the Church to gain vocations would be to focus on second-careerists. These retired professionals, mature and experienced, might just be ideal candidates for the priesthood. But the drawback here is that most of these men are married with children and therefore unordainable. Even the unmarried ones would have to spend 4-6 years in the seminary by today's standards and have precious few years to serve as priests. There is not much real help or hope here.

If parish priests and Catholic parents no longer are enthusiastic about promoting vocations, if the Church is unwilling to even discuss a married clergy, male or female, then what can the Church do to provide sufficient ministers for all the tomorrows? The Church leaders can and should do what virtually every institution, large and small, does to buy and sell, recruit and attract attention. The Bishops should advertise!

The US military forces provide a stellar example. When the US government abolished the universal draft after the Vietnam War on January 17, 1973, the Pentagon faced the tough task of filling the ranks of the army, navy and air force with able-bodied volunteers. The top brass succeeded in satisfying their quotas only by advertising. Radio and TV, billboards and placards began to fill the American scene with messages such as "Be All You Can Be", "Army Strong", "The Few, the Proud, the Marines". Advertising was the key.

The US Army spent 666 million on advertising in 2012. But this figure is dwarfed by major corporations. General Foods spent 1.002 billion to advertise its array of products in 2013. Microsoft outlaid 2.5 billion in 2013 to sell you the latest Windows device and more. Coca Cola put out 2.9 billion in 2011 to promote its latest soft drink. How much did the Catholic Church spend on recruiting in 2013? Precious little if anything, I'm afraid.

Yet the Catholic Church is the largest non-profit institution in the USA. It operates in virtually every city and town in the Country. It has the largest college and university system in the world. Its professional manpower, the priests, is shrinking in numbers daily for the lack of replacements, vocations and seminarians. The CEO's of the Church, the Bishops can act today to augment their priestly ranks, if only they would advertise.

By sheer dint of his position, the parish priest is a true generator of wealth. As we mentioned earlier, the pastor of a large parish of 3 or 4 thousand faithful generates many millions of dollars during his career. These funds go to support numerous causes, from local soup kitchens to maintenance of the bishop's Chancery. If a million dollars in advertising produces only one priest a year, the bishop is still way ahead of the financial game. It's a win-win proposition.

It is pretty much a given that priests no longer promote the priesthood to the younger generation as they once did. Several reasons are usually proffered for this loss of zeal that earlier marked the working priesthood. The child-abuse scandal, closing of parishes, aging of the corps of clergy, dissatisfaction with leadership – all contribute to the low morale among today's priests. But there is one sure-fire way to raise the self-image of the priesthood, an easy and relatively inexpensive way. And that is to advertise. A multi-media blitz on the challenge and nobility of the priesthood would do wonders to raise the self-esteem of today's clergy.

Let's just say that the Bishops decide to give advertising a try to boost vocations in the Church. A delegation of five Hierarchs visits Madison Avenue, NYC to interview at Omni-Media, INC, the largest firm on the block. The Vice President of Marketing, Mr. Simon Kaufman asks the Bishops to tell him something about their institution. The senior Cardinal begins. "Our Church is 2,000 years old, the largest non-profit in the world. Our Founder was God Himself in the person of His one Son, Jesus, who early on chose a Board of Directors of 12 Jewish men, one of whom, Simon Peter was named CEO. This same Peter soon moved our headquarters to Rome, the largest city of the world. We have since grown to claim some 1.2 billion members with operations in every country and city of the world. Now, however, we need more ministers and can't seem to inspire enough candidates. Can you help us, Mr. Kaufman?"

The ad agent looks quizzically at the bishops and, after a brief pause, moves his chair closer to his putative clients to ask a final question: "Exactly what kind of advertising have you been using?" The Bishops look at each other, hesitating to respond. Finally, one brave soul blurts out "None".

And so the deal is made, as handshakes and high hopes abound. A national blitzkrieg of advertising soon appears with TV and radio spots in major markets, billboards on the Interstates, a national hotline for inquiries, placards for every church, chapel and religious school in the USA. Early indications were the ad campaign was working.

Last week, I was driving southward on US 95 toward Philadelphia, when I noticed that the traffic was slowing down ahead. The cars were creeping along in the right lane and the passengers were pointing excitedly to a newly erected billboard. As I approached the sign I saw a giant-sized priest, about 30 years old, smiling down on the traffic with piercing blue eyes and wavy brown hair. In bold black letters the text read: "CHECK YOUR MESSAGES #YOU MIGHT HAVE THE CALL´ At the bottom of the billboard there was a national vocation hotline phone number" 1-800-GOD-CALL.

****

PS While this book is trademarked, all the ideas are free for the taking.

CHAPTER VII

WOMEN IN THE CHURCH

❧━━━━☙

When sultry song stylist Sarah Vaughan sang "It's a Man's World" from her 1967 album, everyone understood what she was saying, but very few people knew that times were about to change. American women were about to embark on a peaceful revolution that, in a few decades, would result in full equality in all areas of society, all, that is, except one, the Catholic Church. If Ms. Vaughan were singing today, she could hit the Billboard's Top Ten with a blockbuster song called "It's a Man's Church".

It's not that women do not participate in the life of the Church. They attend the services, receive the Sacraments, raise their children with Sunday School classes, First Communion, Confirmation and Catholic education. On the parish level women donate their funds, work in the church kitchens, lead the rosary society and clean the church. Women are active in the Church. What they lack, however, is what today psychologists call "Voice". In the realm of authority, i.e. decision-making of the Church, women are non-existent.

This chapter is not a brief for the ordination of women priests or, God forbid, women bishops! That decision can be made only by those far above me in rank and rule. The main concern here is that when any society bars one half of its population, a priori, from its structure of authority, that society will be less than fair and much less than successful in its mission. The Church has a long history of dealing unfairly with women, a history that must be understood and overcome.

As early as the 2nd century, Church Fathers wrote about the "inferior nature" of women. Clement of Alexandria in his "Paedagogus" (2:33) said that women should be ashamed of their female nature. The North African Tertullian opined that women, as daughters of Eve, are the doors by which the Evil One enters ("De Cultu Feminarum", Ch. I). The writers lived in the heady matrix of Hellenistic misogynism, which followed Aristotle in regarding women as deformed males and liars by nature.

St. John Chrysostom (c. 347-407) wrote "On the Priesthood" in 386, right after his ordination, and says that "When someone has to preside over the Church and be entrusted with the care of so many souls, then let all woman-kind give way before the magnitude of the task…" (2, 2). Commenting on I Timothy (II:12-15), John proffers the rationale for the "inferiority" of women in Homily IX: "The male sex enjoys the higher honor, for man was formed first and is due superior status. For the woman Eve once taught the man Adam and made him guilty of disobedience, and she wrought our ruin."

With the appearance in the West of "scientific" Aristotelism in the 13th century Christian writers reaffirmed the debased nature of women. Albertus Magnus, the mentor of Thomas Aquinas, wrote that woman is a misbegotten man and has a defective nature…"and so one should guard against every woman, as if she were a deadly viper and horned devil." (Commentary on Aristotle", No. 15).

The Father of scholastic philosophy and theology, St. Thomas Aquinas (1225-1275) held that women's only purpose on earth was to give birth. In his masterwork "The Summa Theologica" Thomas writes that "we are told that woman was made to be a help to man, but she was not fitted to help a man except in generation, because another man would have proved to be a more effective help in anything else." (Q. 98, Art. 2). Discoursing on the virtue of sobriety is the "Summa" the Angelic Doctor held that "sobriety is most requisite in the young and in women, because concupiscence of pleasure thrives in the young on account of the heat of youth, while in women there is not sufficient strength of mind to resist concupiscence." (Q. 149, Art. 4). These sentiments echoed throughout Western schools, seminaries and chanceries for centuries.

These early Christian writers gave voice to the basic elements of Christian anthropology, the study of the origin, nature and destiny of all Christians, even all of mankind. Platonism was the main pagan source for the earliest of these Fathers, while Aristotle served this purpose during the late Middle Ages. Platonic idealism held that the mind ("Nous") is the highest and most divine-like quality in humans and can be found only in males. Females are characterized by the bodily passions and emotions, which by nature make them inferior to males. Plato's student Aristotle was more a realist than an idealist but still believed in man's superiority over women. Aristotle's hierarchy of beings reads "God-Spirits-Man-Woman-Non Humans-Matter", according to Rosemary Radford Ruether in "Sexism and God-Talk", (1983), p. 79.

On the basis of the Greek anthropology formulated by Plato, Aristotle and their followers, the early Christian think-ers built their edifice of the Church's outlook on man's/woman's place in the world. First the Christian Fathers studied the Genesis accounts of creation and concluded that the Greeks were indeed correct, because man was created by God before woman, man's rib was the material of women's creation and woman's purpose was to be a helpmate for man. Then the Fathers studied St. Paul and determined that women are to be subjected to men, be silent in church (1 Cor. 14:34), receive instruction silently and under complete control. I do not permit a woman to teach or to have authority over a man. She must be quiet. (1 Tim. 3:11-13). The first Christian writers were convinced that women by nature itself were inferior to and under the domination of men. If women by both Edenic origin and nature itself are inferior to men, who are full participants in the "Imago Dei" and so destined to return someday to God in Heaven, then what are women's eschatological hopes? Did not Christ gain salvation for both men and women? Of course, say the Fathers. But women share in the redemptive promise of Christ's death and resurrection mainly and only by being faithful helpmates to men and bringing forth new life as mothers. As Ruether explains: "Aquinas concluded that woman, although defective and misbegotten in her individual nature, nevertheless belongs to the overall 'perfection' of nature because of her role in procreation." (Ruether, op. cit., p. 96)

Theology has consequences. By the end of the Middle Ages the inferiority of women vis-a-vis men and the former's unworthiness to serve in any leadership role in the Church were firmly established in practice. There would be no female priests, no married priests, not even female altar-servers. In fact, women were even forbidden to approach the altar because of their ritual impurity. The 1917 Code of Church laws bans women from entering the sanctuary and "they may give responses only from afar." (Canon 813).

Theology sometimes has deadly consequences. While St. Augustine (354-430) believed that Satan could not control the lives of humans and transform them into diabolical witches, his equally influential and much later fellow-theologian St. Thomas Aquinas (1275-1275) did so believe. Douglas Linder writes that "Aquinas argued that demons had the habit of reaping the sperm of men and spreading it among women. In Aquinas' mind sex and witchcraft begin what will become a long association. ("A Brief History of Witchcraft Persecution before Salem", 2005). The theological stage was set for the following centuries. Women and demons were to be linked together as evil-doing partners in the minds of both ecclesiastics and civilians. Such witches were a danger to society and must be punished, thought the late Medieval authorities.

The outbreak of the Catharism movement in southern Europe in the late Middle Ages provided the impetus for the Church to act punitively against those who denied the orthodox teaching on women, sex and marriage. The Council of Tarnovo (1211) decreed: "To those who say that a woman conceives in her belly by the cooperation of Satan, that Satan has resided there and withdraws only at the birth of the child, and that he cannot be put to flight by holy baptism but only by prayer and fasting – to those who speak thus, anathema." (Cited by John T. Noonan Jr., "Contraception", Harvard University Press, 1986, p. 189) The Church was convinced that its teaching on marriage was under attack by the Cathars and the nexus of women-sex-Satan was the enemy.

The Cathars were gradually defeated by Church and civil authorities, who burned their villages in France and Italy, executed their leaders and excommunicated their sympathizers. However, many followers of this dualistic and antinomian lifestyle escaped to Germany and the Savoy. It was in these regions that the witchcraft trials of women erupted into history around 1450.

The Pope most closely linked to leading the battle against witches is Innocent VIII, who issued the papal bull "Summis desiderantes" in 1484 directing the Inquisition to pursue and try all suspected witches. Innocent commissioned two monks, Heinrich Kramer and Jacob Sprenger to compile a full report on witchcraft activity in Germany, France and Italy. By 1486 the report "Malleus Maleficarum" ("The Hammer of Witches") was completed and became a handbook for all witch-hunters. This work gives us a pellucid insight into the Church's attitude toward women at the close of the Middle Ages, as can be seen in the following passage cited by Ruether (op. cit., p. 170):

> As for the first question, why a greater number of witches is found in the fragile feminine sex than among men, is indeed a fact that it were idle to contradict…Since women are feebler in both mind and body, it is not surprising that they should come under the spell of witchcraft. For as regards intellect, of the understanding of spiritual things, they seem to be of a different nature from men…But the natural reason is that she is more carnal than a man, as is clear from her many carnal abominations. And it should be noted that there was a defect in the forma-tion of the first woman, since she was formed from a bent rib, that is, a rib of the breast which is bent as it were in a contrary direction to a man. And since through this defect she is an imperfect animal, she always deceives…And all this is indicated by the etymology of the word, for "Femina" comes from "Fe" and "Minus",

since she is ever weaker to hold and preserve the faith. Therefore a wicked woman is by her nature quicker to waver in her faith and consequently quicker to adjure the faith, which is the root of witchcraft.

With "Malleus Maleficarum" in hand, the witch hunters spread throughout Europe and executed some 50,000 to 80,000 "witches", about 80% of whom were women, reports Douglas Linder (op. cit., p. 5). Hundreds of thousands of others were tried and either punished, confined or released. It is to be noted that the newly established Protestant churches shared and sometimes exceeded the zeal of their Catholic brethren in persecuting suspected witches during the 1500's.

Of course, there is no one cause for the complex phenomenon of the medieval fury of witch-hunting in Europe. Scholars have mentioned such causative elements as general superstition, common ignorance of sexual and procreative processes, strange meteorological events, misunderstanding of physical and psychological diseases and other unexplained factors. But it is clear that the underlying framework and justification for the witch-hunters can be found in the anthropological theology of the churches, both Catholic and Protestant. Simply put, women were inferior in mind, body and soul.

The rise of Humanism in the 1500's began to delimit the witch hysteria, while the Enlightment in the late 1600's brought about its end. An old woman named Temperance Lloyd had the dubious distinction of being the last person in England to be executed in 1682 for witchcraft, reports Douglas Linder (op. cit., p. 7). But the fate of women in the Western World was by no means secure, for their inferior status in society remained in force. Somewhat akin to the half-life of a radio-active isotope, the lot of women went from outright persecution to hostility and finally to simple inequality in the West. The prejudice against women diminished but never died.

A brief look at women's suffrage in the USA illustrates this abiding bias against women. The US Constitution of 1789 did not address the issue of voting rights, but all states banned women from the vote except New Jersey. But even the Garden State repealed women's suffrage in1807. Susan B. Anthony and Elizabeth Cady Stanton drafted a women's suffrage amendment in 1878. It took 41 years before the Nineteenth Amendment was passed in 1920 to allow women the right to vote. The first woman elected to the US Senate was Ophelia W. Caraway of Arkansas as late as 1938. The first woman to sit on the US Supreme Court was Sandra Day O'Connor only in 1981.

The history of women's suffering in the USA began in Salem, MA with the European settlement (1620) and the theology that accompanied these Puritans on the Mayflower. While the Salem witch-hunts may be long gone, the theology of male supremacy has perdured for centuries in American society. Only today, in the 21st century are women approaching full equality with men in all societal spheres, except one, the Church.

Pope John Paul II, now a canonized saint, wrote an Apostolic Letter called "Mulieris Dignitatem" in 1988, a theological paean on the dignity of women. The lengthy letter covered nine chapters and 116 pages in the US Catholic Conference edition. It is difficult to tell what effect, if any, this worthy work had on the fate of women in the world. But suppose the same Pope had instead appointed Mother Teresa to be a Cardinal, "causa honoris", of the Roman Church. Every newspaper in the world would have front-paged this story. Virtually every woman in the world would welcome the news with a smile and the thought: "Finally we have our voice".

Pope Francis, the latest holder of St. Peter's Throne, startled the Catholic world in an interview published March 5, 2014. Speaking about the role of women in authoritative positions of the Church, the Pontiff affirmed that "women must have a greater role in the leadership of the Catholic Church. It's true that women can and must be more present in Church decision-making." The entire interview appeared in Italy's "Corriere Della Sera" and was quoted by Bloomberg News in the "New York Post" of March 6, 2014. What is of great interest here is the Pope's choice of words "can" and "must". In other words, women have the ability, just like men, to sit in the high councils of the Church. And secondly, it is not simply an option for bishops to appoint women to important positions. The Hierarchs simply should and must do so.

Major US Dioceses have a countless number of committees, councils, conferences, boards and ministries. All these units have vital work to do that affects all the faithful. Yet, some of these commissions are all-male, while others have a token woman on board. One must wonder how effective these units can be with no real female representation, especially since women's issues often dominate many of these commissions?

The sex-abuse scandal devastated the Church's finances and morale, as well as its public image, in recent years. The many and often wrong decisions of Chancery officials were made primarily by men. Again, one must wonder if things would have turned out differently if women had a voice in the Chanceries throughout America? Perhaps this issue alone was enough to prompt Pope Francis to insist that women must be included in the decision-making of the Church? One Hierarch of a large Eastern-rite Church appointed a female Chancellor in the 1980"s, who served with distinction and integrity for about 20 years. During her tenure not one case of clergy sex-abuse of minors was reported. Of course it could have been just good luck. But then again it might have been the watchful eyes of a woman at the helm.

It is true that Our Lord chose twelve men as His Apostles, His closest advisors. But when the going got tough on that first Good Friday, only one man, the Beloved John remained at His side. It is also true that Our Lord had many female followers and confidantes, such as sisters Martha and Mary, and the women at the Cross. Matthew's Gospel reads: "And many women were there, watching from a distance, the same women who had followed Jesus from Galilee and looked after Him. Among them were Mary Magdala, Mary the mother of James and Joseph, and the mother of Zebedee's sons." (27: 55-56).

Countless such modern-day Marys and Marthas are capable and willing to "look after" Our Lord and His Holy Church today. It only remains for the Bishops to invite them into the Chancery door.

CHAPTER VIII

THE PARISH PRIEST

◦━━━━━◦

M ichael was the ideal seminarian. His twelve years of seminary training prepared him to be obedient to his superiors and faithful to his prayer-life. He was athletic and studious and got along well with both the "jocks" and the "nerds" in his class. When ordination time arrived in the spring of 1967, Michael was ready and able. Enthused with the after-glow of Vatican II, the ground-breaking Ecumenical Council (1962-1965), Michael excitedly accepted his first priestly posting as assistant pastor in a suburb of New York City.

Father Michael was the ideal priest. He practiced and preached the Gospel with the fervor of a freshly-minted minister of Christ and was embraced warmly by both the old pastor and the faithful. Michael was a happy priest. He was even happier when he met Maria, the young and single parish secretary. This later happiness soon turned to love in Michael's 27-year-old heart. After only one year in the priesthood the rookie priest decided to leave his calling and marry Maria. He broke a lot of hearts to follow the stirrings of his own hungry heart.

Michael did not know, nor did anyone else at the time, that he was at the leading edge of a alpine avalanche of priestly departures from the active ministry. Hundreds if not thousands of priests quit their calling in the aftermath of Vatican II. So many priests left the ministry in the 1960's and 1970s that the current number of diocesan priests in the USA, about 27,000, is still some 40% less than the high-water mark of last century.

In spite of all the holy hoopla attached to the Vatican II Council about reform and renewal, the post-conciliar period was not a very joyful one for Catholics, priests and laity alike. It is clear that the priests, like my friend Michael, were most disturbed by the June 24, 1967 encyclical "Sacerdotalis caelibatus" of Pope Paul VI, which reaffirmed the celibacy discipline for all Roman Catholic priests. The high hopes, theologically well-founded, of many if not most clergy were dashed by this letter, which brought about a personal crisis for the men. The resulting effect of this missive was a weakened resolve, especially among the younger priests, to remain in the ministry. So the clergy, feeling betrayed by their superiors, left their calling in droves. Even the older clerics, who "toughed it out" and stayed at their posts, were not particularly happy with the above developments, at least not happy enough to continue to recruit new seminarians from among their parish youth. The vocation shortage, soon to become the priest shortage, has its roots in the Church of the 1970's and 1980's.

While the personal morale of the priests was seriously wounded by the celibacy encyclical, it was the encyclical of the following year that hurt their professional well-being. This shocking event came in the form of the July 25, 1968, encyclical "Humanae vitae" by the same Pontiff, Pope Paul VI.

This papal document reaffirmed the traditional Catholic teaching opposing all forms of birth control with the sole exception of the so-called "rhythm method". In a word, while the priests and laity were looking for a "change", all they got was the same old. To illustrate the depth of discontent on this issue, Father Andrew Greeley pointed out in "The Catholic Myth" (p. 23) that "in 1963 half the Catholic population had accepted the birth-control teaching. In 1974 only 12 percent accepted it." Today it is even less than that.

While the laity struggled with their conscience over the contraception ban and eventually decided to ignore it, the priests were afloat in a totally different boat. This Encyclical placed the priests squarely between two irreconcilable forces with no out in sight. On the one hand the clergy had vowed obedience to the teaching authority of the Church, i.e. to uphold "Humanae vitae". But on the other hand, they heard from their faithful that these Catholics would not and could not follow the Pope's instruction. Some priests tried to teach and even preach on the "evils" of contraception, but they had little or no success. Other priests fell silent on the subject, hoping that time and common sense would bring resolution. All the priests, however, felt some degree of frustration if not outright anger. They were in a professional dilemma not of their own making and were not happy about it at all. These clergymen asked, often silently but sometimes aloud, variations of two questions. Where is the good will of the laity? Where is the good sense of the Church?

The parish priest has always been the heart and soul of the Church. Daily he calls the faithful to prayer and praise, comforts the bereaved, rejoices with his newly-weds, preaches and teaches the Gospel of Christ in good times and bad. He maintains the buildings, ministers to the sick, keeps the books, cares for the poor and hungry. He even sends substantial parish funds to his Bishop and Pope on a regular basis. To do all this and more the priest needs the support of his flock and his bishop. In today's betroubled Church the priest needs such support more than ever.

Two fairly recent phenomena have transpired in the Church to seriously wound the already low morale of the USA priests. The first is the clergy sex abuse scandal. In May of 2013 The United States Conference of Catholic Bishops reported 16,795 cases of child abuse by clerics. More than 6,300 clergymen were charged with abusing children by either civil or church authorities in recent years. These statistics cover the timeframe of 1950-2012. The decade of 1975-1985 saw the greatest percentage of incidents involving the sexual abuse of children by clerics. In many cases bishops simply transferred suspected priests to new parishes, where the abuse began anew.

Chief among the victims of this scandal were, of course, the children themselves, along with their parents, families and friends. The Church itself suffered, both in its public image and purse. By 2012 some three billion dollars have been lost to the Church in legal fees, awards and sundry other expenses.

But also among the victims were the 95% of good and faithful priests, who are suffering still today from the blowback of this scandal, caused by 5% of their wayward brothers. Prudent priests curtailed their meetings with the altar servers and sodality girls. Teenager excursions to the beach or the mountains with Father Pastor are non-existent. All the priests have had their good characters silently questioned, when out in public, by a furtive glance of a passerby. Some clergy reported receiving catcalls of vulgar derision on the street. The morale or job satisfaction of the clergy has taken a serious hit from the current crisis of the abuse of children by derelict priests and the subsequent inaction of their superiors.

Pope Francis himself expressed outrage when informed that two percent of the world's Catholic clerics were active pedophiles. There are some 400,000 priests worldwide, which translates into about 8,000 abusers of children. The available USA statistics, as reported by the USCCB and BishopAccountability.org in 2013, indicate that about five percent of American clerics were found guilty of child abuse in recent decades. In the interview with the Italian newspaper "La Republica" published July 13, 2014, the Pope called pedophilia "a leprosy present in our house". Both the "New York Post" and the "New York Daily News" published lengthy articles on the Pope's interview on Monday, July 14, 2014. In the middle of the interview Pope Francis was quoted as saying that "among the 2% who are pedophiles are priests, bishops and cardinals. Others, more numerous, know but keep quiet.....I find this state of affairs intolerable."

The good God-workers in the Church, especially the priests, also find this abuse scandal intolerable and heartbreaking. But compounding this heartache for the priests (and the laity as well) is another recent development, that of parish closures. No sane and sober soul would object to closing a parish that is realistically nonviable. If St. Prudentia Parish has precious little funds and mostly empty pews on Sunday, it's time to say "goodbye" to the aged parish. But this is not the case with many if not most closed parishes.

The Center for Applied Research in the Apostolate (CARA) at Georgetown University reported that as of January 1, 2014, some 2,137 parishes were closed since 1990. And these closings continue apace today. The pastors of these closed parishes were simply informed, after years if not decades of dedicated ministry, to move on to another parish. It's a safe bet that their hearts were broken, their spirits crushed, their morale shattered. What's to guarantee, the transferred priests must be asking, that their new parish would not be shuttered a few years down the road?

Another negative fallout from closing parishes is the doubling of work for a new pastor. The typical transferred priest-pastor from a closed parish is assigned a much larger parish community, double or treble the size of his former posting. This increased burden on the average USA priest, age 58, can be a true professional hardship at this stage in his life. A major East-coast Archdiocese now uses the figure of 5,000 as the number of faithful every priest is expected to serve. The priest shortage is the major reason given for closing parishes. Yet only 68% of diocesan priests is active in the parish ministry, according to the CARA report mentioned above. What are these other clerics doing? Chancery office work? Academic work? Sick leave? If able-bodied and not suspended, these men could and should be assigned parish ministry.

The main solution to the priest shortage is well-known in 3,496 USA parishes, where a lay person or religious serves as the parish administrator in the absence of a resident priest. As we write at length about these priest-less parishes in another chapter, this solution has been tried and found satisfactory primarily in the West and South. It needs to be implemented in the Northern and Eastern dioceses of the USA to obviate the professional burnout of the overburdened pastors.

Fortunately, we have on hand a scientific survey on this subject of the morale and job satisfaction of priests in the USA. This landmark study was presented to the Society for the Scientific Study of Religious in Portland, Oregon on October 20, 2006 under the title "Satisfaction and Morale Among Parish Clergy". The work was authored by Dean R. Hoge of the Catholic University of America and Alexey S. Krindatch of the Patriarch Athenagoras Orthodox Institute/ Graduate Theological Union. The authors compared the morale of Roman Catholic priests with that of two Orthodox jurisdictions in the USA. The results are revealing as both a comparative study and as a stand-alone picture of the clergy in either church.

Table 1 of the Survey concerned the sources of satisfaction in the life and work of priests. Some 95% of Catholic priests responded that their greatest source of satisfaction was the celebration of the liturgy (the Mass) and sacraments, while 80% replied that preaching the Word was of "great importance". Not of great importance for a majority of the priests were: parish administration (35%), respect to the priestly office (23%) and social reform ministry (21%).

The Survey's Table 4 is most relevant to this chapter on priests, since it discusses the sources of support for the parish clergy. About 60% of priests-respondents asserted that they receive "strong support" from their families, 54% from their staff members, 50% from their parishioners. At the low end, only 29% mentioned receiving strong support from their bishops, 28% from their fellow priests, 11% from the Vatican and a negligible 3% from the NCCB. Then asked about their problems, the Catholic priests mentioned three major concerns. Table 6 showed that, in the response to the question of what might be a "great problem" in your ministry, the highest number of priests (25%) listed the exercise of authority in the Church. About 22% mentioned "too much work" and some 18% answered "unrealistic demands of the laity".

In a very revelatory survey section entitled Chart 1, the priests were asked to agree or disagree with three statements. Some 72% of Catholic clergymen agreed, strongly or somewhat, that the Church needs to move faster to empower the laity in ministry. About 46% agreed that the priests ought to be able to choose their own bishop and 23% said that parishes should choose their own pastors.

The final survey section, Table 10, lists the issues that the Catholic clergy feel should be openly and more fully discussed. Under the rubric "very important to me", these problem areas were: the image of priesthood (64%), sharing ministry with laity (49%), emotional maturity of priests (46%), the problem of overwork (46%), the process of selecting bishops (40%).

To summarize the results of this survey of Catholic priests, it is clear that the clergy find their highest job satisfactions at the altar, celebrating the services and preaching the Word of God. Two related areas of high dissatisfaction for the priests were the low level of support they received from their bishops and the Vatican, as well as how church authority is exercised. Other major problems for the clergy were: overwork, the slow pace of empowerment of the laity in ministry and the poor public image of the priesthood.

There is no reason to believe that these negative numbers have improved since this survey was published in 2006. There is every reason to think that the morale of the Catholic clergy has worsened since then, because the clergy sex scandal has now blossomed into a full-blown crisis and the parish closure phenomenon is now an epidemic. The priests could only helplessly stand fast in the epicenter of these religious storms as the tornadic winds ripped apart their self-esteem and morale.

The key to preserving or, in many cases, restoring the morale of parish priests is the support of the faithful, for it is with their parishioners that priests have daily and immediate contact. Such support can bolster the self-image of the clergy, create an atmosphere of respect in the community for them and motivate them to continue their salvific ministry among their assigned flocks.

In both actions and words this support can be given in many diverse ways. Complimentary words on a sermon, smiles and handshakes after services, friendly greetings on the street or at the supermarket – all send a powerful message of support to Father. The parish bulletin board should list Father Pastor's birthday and anniversary dates to remind the faithful to send along a card, with or without a token gift. One elderly pastor told me he receives literally hundreds of greeting cards from his faithful every Christmas and Easter. After the tough and tedious holyday services this old pastor reads through all his cards, in the loneliness of the now stilled rectory, with a smile and even a happy tear in his eye, knowing that he is appreciated and loved by his people.

But even with the good support of his parish, a priest may struggle mightily with his ministerial mind-set and morale, if he does not receive the full support of his bishop. In theory this lack of support is hard to understand. After all, the bishop is like the CEO of a large corporation and is dependent on the success of his local managers, the priests. If these latter falter and fail, the head of the organization will ultimately fail as well. The bishop is dependent on the parish priests for cultivating vocations, raising funds, implementing programs, teaching the faith and morals of the Church. In the truest of sense, the success of the parish priests becomes the success of their bishop. Many bishops understand this. Some do not. It might be worthwhile to point out several bishops who "get it" and offer strong support to their clergymen.

One Eastern Church Hierarch sends out letters to his priests every spring informing them of his plan to transfer some clergy in the fall. He asks the priests plainly to write him if they would consider moving to another parish. The parish priests appreciate this good-will gesture and respond accordingly, for they feel they have some "voice" in their professional life.

A Roman Catholic bishop keeps a list of all the retired and ailing priests from the diocese. Every Christmas and Easter he sends them all a hand-written card with a substantial check from his personal account. For weeks in advance the retirement-home clergymen excitedly discuss among themselves how they plan to spend this regular windfall.

Another Eastern Church bishop, now retired, has a list of the anniversary of ordination dates of his former priests. He makes a personal phone call to every priest on his special day to thank him for his service to the Church. This independently wealthy bishop is known for his generosity to cash-starving parishes. A classmate told us recently of a large cash gift this bishop made to a poor parish in Pennsylvania.

One newly appointed Latin Bishop spent his first week in office memorizing the names of all his priests and their parishes. This caring hierarch starts his in-office day by making one phone call to a surprised pastor, inquiring about the priest's health and happiness.

Another Archbishop makes it his business to seek out former priests who have left the active ministry. He typically offers his help, financial or otherwise, and succeeded in bringing back several of these men into the priestly fold.

These and untold other hierarchs understand that their support is vital for the morale and psychological welfare of their presbyterate. And they also see that they the bishops, as well as their parishes, depend for their own wellbeing on a corps of clergymen, who "feed the sheep and lambs" in good times and bad.

Some 45 years ago, as a newly ordained priest, I was drafted unexpectedly to drive the aging Archbishop to a church 100 miles away in the wilds of Pennsylvania's mountains. It seems the regular chauffeur had taken ill that Sunday morning. The Hierarch was scheduled to celebrate the 50th anniversary of the church's founding with a solemn pontifical liturgy at 12 noon with some twenty local priests and hundreds of faithful. The drive was uneventful for the first 50 miles or so until we hit a detour sign and had to navigate on the back roads. It wasn't long before we became hopelessly lost! As the clock ticked down the good Archbishop began to yell at me, first in English, then in Ukrainian and finally in a language I could not identify. Finally God's tender mercy intervened in the person of a roadside bicyclist who agreed to lead us onto the main road to the Church. We arrived only five minutes late and the Hierarch grumpily hastened to his episcopal duties. On the way home an eerie silence filled the black Benz, as I contemplated an early end to my priestly career. Once back at the episcopal residence I carried the bishop's bags into the foyer and started to leave. He told me to wait a second as he handed me a crumpled-up ten-dollar bill. His parting words I will never forget: "Son, your chauffeuring days are over, but your priestly days are just starting. God bless you."

Chapter IX

The Church and Youth

"Father, we need a bigger bus," someone screamed from the middle of the pack of 90 Philadelphia teenagers trying to board the 75-passenger chartered Greyhound. The Pastor "volunteered" his station wagon to handle the extra teens to forestall the incipient riot and the youth soon embarked on their annual ski-trip to the Poconos in Northeast Pennsylvania. With two young curates as chaperones and the prospect of deep powder in the mountains, the center-city teens were bursting with excitement this snowy Friday evening. What more could they ask? They were with their friends and their beloved priests heading to the high country for a weekend of skiing and singing, good food and drink, and the outside chance of stealing a kiss or two with their special someone before the fireplace in the cozy lodge. The priests were savvy enough to go to bed early Saturday evening so as not to act as watchdogs over the hyperactive teens. After all, the good Fathers had to rise early Sunday to celebrate the Liturgy in the main hall of the lodge for all the youth.

This scene and countless variations of it were played out weekly in most US parishes in the 1960's and 1970's. There were Friday night dances, Saturday afternoon basketball or volleyball games, Wednesday evening meetings, weekend car washes and yard sales to raise funds for the youth. There were national conventions of the Catholic Youth Organization (CYO) and the League of Ukrainian Catholic Youth (LUCY). Back in the day Catholic youth were well served, shepherded through their turbulent teens by thousands of youth ministers and caring clerics. A steel bond was forged in prior years between the Church and the youth, thanks mainly to the hard work of the sisters in the schools and the priests in the parishes. This relationship remained in place as the same young Catholics were later married in church, baptized their children in church and raised their families within the confines of the Faith. In their youth they amassed a ton of "social capital", the sum total of all their positive contacts and relationships, which provided them with a lasting formation. All their lives they would remember the happy days and times of their youth spent in and around the Church.

Perhaps a few personal narratives will add some depth to the above lines! The first concerns a relatively unknown medical professional. The second involves a world-renowned rock star.

Joseph K. was a passenger on the ski-bus mentioned in our opening paragraph. He was a ghetto kid from the mean streets of North Philadelphia, but he found comfort and joy with his friends in the church's programs for the local youth. Joe was inspired by the young priests to finish high-school and pursue a career in medicine. After many years of part-time study, he graduated as a nurse-anesthetist and practices today in Allentown, Pa., where he attends Church. He recently remarked that "Father R. saved him from the street".

Bruce Springsteen, arguably the greatest living rock star, was born in 1949 and lived in Freehold, NJ. Along with his

E Street Band, he has entertained countless millions on the five populated continents. He lived out his youthful days next to St. Rose of Lima Church in Freehold, where he and his extended family attended. He was a "handful" for the sisters in the Parish Elementary School, but they never gave up on him. For his 2013 concert at the Meadowlands in East Rutherford, NJ "The Boss", as he is known by his multitude of fans, provided free passes for all the nuns and priests still serving at St. Rose Church. His explanation to the 60 thousand in attendance for the clerical VIP's in the front row: "Once a Catholic, always a Catholic".

But times have now changed, no doubt for the worse, in regard the Church and youth. In 1970 there were 9,366 Catholic elementary schools in the US according to the Center of Applied Research in the Apostolate (CARA). Today, 2014, there are some 5,858 such schools still open. And more are closing every year. The picture of Catholic high schools is the same. In 1970 about 2,000 such schools were educating the youth of this country. This number has fallen to 1,340 today. Fewer schools mean fewer educated young Catholics. The end result is a weakened link between the youth and the Church, a link not likely to hold during the inevitable turbulence of college, marriage and child-bearing.

Back in the day, when young Catholics were asked where they lived in the city, they had the habit of replying with the name of the parish and school rather than the street address. For example, a Philadelphia youth would respond "St. Peter's Church", if he/she lived on Girard Avenue. But this is no longer the case. The link is going if not already gone.

Of course, the decline of professional manpower and womanpower in the Church is a dominant factor in its ability to reach out to today's youth. The CARA report indicates that there were some 60,000 priests serving about 47 million

Catholics in the US as of 1970. Today, the figures are 40,000 priests in service for about 68 million faithful. In the span of two generations the number of clerics declined by 34%, while the number of parishioners increased some 41%. Religious sisters are facing even more drastic declines throughout their various congregations. There were 160,931 sisters ministering in the US in 1970. Today that number has shrunk to about 57,000. What is most telling about these statistical realities is that the decline continues today. The "Catholic Almanac" reports that in 2010 there were 729 fewer priests and 1,714 fewer nuns ministering in the US than there were in 2009.

This numerical decline in both male and female ministers certainly bodes ill for the Church's future in the US. It only compounds several other problems for the Church, such as the clergy abuse scandal, the closing of parishes, and the financial health of the various ecclesial entities. There is no doubt that hard times lie ahead for the Church, especially in its outreach and retention efforts. A special victim of these current organizational woes will probably be the Church's ministry to the youth.

The Pew Research Center in Washington, DC is the premier collector and interpreter of statistical data on churches in the US today. The widely available 2009-2010 Pew Report is an eye-opener for any serious inquirer on the status of the Catholic Church today. The lead story (p. 9) reads: "One-in-ten American adults is a former Catholic". This translates to some 25 million Americans who have left the Church. About half this number joined a Protestant church, while the other half remained unaffiliated. The main reasons given by these "lost sheep" were: dissatisfaction with Catholic social teaching on birth control, homosexuality, abortion and treatment of women, as well as with the Catholic teaching about the Bible.

Some 30% of former Catholics say they left because they were unhappy with the priests at their parish.

The same Pew Report (p. 21) informs us that in the current churn of members to/from a given religion in America, the Catholic Church has lost the most members. Those who have left the Church outnumber its converts by a margin of four-to-one. The retention rate of childhood faithful is about 68% in the Church. Of those who left the Church about 15% have become Protestant and another 15% became unaffiliated. The three common reasons for leaving the Church and joining a Protestant church or becoming unattached are reported in the Pew survey (p. 24) as: spiritual needs not being met, rejection of the Church's teaching and drifting away from the Church.

In regard the Church's ministry to the youth, three findings in the Pew Report deserve the attention of all Church leaders. Of all born-and-raised Catholics only about 30% attend services at least monthly. Another 40% are nominal Catholics and seldom or never attend. The final 30% have left the Church. The second relevant finding is that membership in a youth group or Sunday School program is no guarantee today that these youth will remain in the Church. Thirdly, only about 50% of adult Catholics and 40% of young Catholics (18-29) believe in a personal God, with Whom they can have a relationship.

A recent study of the religious practices and attitudes of the Millennials, the cohort of youth born in the 1990's, sheds much light on the current and near-term status of youth in the Church. This survey was completed in 2012 by a joint effort of the Public Religion Research Institute and the Berkley Center for Religion, Peace and World Affairs of Georgetown University. These researchers found that only two-thirds (64%) of Millennials, who were raised Catholic, remain within the Faith. About 43% of Catholic Millennials reported that they seldom or never attend services in church. While a large majority (76%) of Millennials affirm that the Church has "good values and principles", a strong majority also felt that the Church is "hypocritical", "judgmental" and "anti-gay".

With such statistical and attitudinal data in evidence, it is clear that today's Church leaders face a daunting challenge to stem the "soul-drain" of youth from the pews on Sunday morning. This task is even more difficult today than in the past because of the aging and diminishing number of clergy (priests and sisters), at work in the parishes. The main component, we are convinced, at any successful out-reach to today's youth has to be the leadership of the laity.

The Catholic bishops understand this. In fact, as far back as 1980 the hierarchs issued the document "Called and Gifted", in which they welcomed the gift "of lay persons who have prepared for professional ministry in the church". Youth ministry was one of these callings expressed by this document. In a follow-up work "Called and Gifted for the Third Millennium" (1995) the US Bishops promised to "expand our study and dialogue concerning lay ministry" in the Church. In a third document "Co-Workers in the Vineyard of the Lord" (2005) the bishops provided a practical roadmap for the training and certification of lay ministers, including those involved in youth ministry.

The success of this national movement to empower the laity is evident in the statistical report of the USCCB, 2014. The number of lay ministers working at least 20 hours per week in paid positions increased about 40% from 1990 to 2005. Today some 30,632 lay ministers are employed in US parishes. About 66% of all churches now have paid lay ministers, many of whom work with youth

Thousands of parishes, however, are too small or too poor to warrant a paid youth minister. Such churches certainly have willing and able married couples, perhaps with teenage children of their own, who can serve as moderators for the parish youth. The on-the-job experience of raising children, especially today's teens, goes a long way in "certifying" a dedicated married couple to work with today's youth.

The National Catholic Young Adult Ministry Association (NCYAMA), based in Washington, DC, provides a myriad of services for youth ministers in the US. This organization offers training services, networking opportunities, job and job bank support, resources and supplies for youth ministers. NCYAMA bills itself as "the national voice for young adult ministry in the United States". Whether with a paid youth minister or a part-time parish volunteer, there is plenty of support available to guarantee a successful youth program in every parish of this country.

While it may be true, as the 2010 Pew Report affirms, that the youth ministry of the Church is no assurance that such youth will remain faithful members of the Church in their adult life, it is nevertheless imperative that today's Church strive to organize its young members. Powerful arguments can be made that the Church has a sacred duty to serve the youth in an organized and universal way.

The first argument is the example of Jesus Christ Himself. He told His Disciples "to let the children come to me" (Mt. 19:14). He cured the young servant of the Centurion (Mt. 8:5), raised up the young daughter of Jairus (Mr. 9:23), fed the men, women and children with loaves and fish (Mt. 14:21) and exorcized the young daughter of the Canaanite Woman (Mt, 15:21). He even chose the youthful brothers James and John (Mt. 4:21) as His Apostles. Any Church leader worth his salt simply must follow Christ and minister to the youth.

Secondly, Church leaders such as recent Popes have issued countless addresses, exhortations, letters and sermons to praise and promote the youth, as well as to urge parents and clergy to teach them of Our Lord and His Holy Church. The most recent effort of the Papacy in this regard was the establishment of World Youth Day, which was first celebrated in Buenos Aires in 1987. Marked every three years, this spiritual festival is next scheduled for 2016 in Poland with the likely attendance of millions of youth and Pope Francis. It is clear from the above that the Church places the highest priority on "letting the children come to me".

The final argument for the need of a robust youth ministry in every diocese and parish of the land comes from the youth themselves. They simply want to know and see the evidence that the modern Church has any care and love for them. The question becomes: How important are the youth in the eyes of the local bishop and pastor? Both words and actions are needed to answer this question.

But all the youth ministry in the world, such as CYO basketball, teen dances, fall hayrides, bowling leagues and even discussion clubs will not guarantee "retention" in the Church. This "R" word, much loved and used by statisticians, indicates that a person remains in the Faith throughout the teen, adult and elderly years. It is clear that the many and tough challenges of adulthood push and pull a person in unforeseen faith-decisions, such as joining another denomination or even becoming unafilliated with any church. The cohort of atheists and agnostics is the fastest growing group among young adults today. Something more than youth activities is needed today to ensure that young Catholics become old Catholics.

This something more goes by the name of discipleship, faith formation or, more recently, evangelization. What all these terms mean is the lasting conviction that Jesus Christ, firstly, is my Brother and Savior. The Church calls us to greet and praise Him, thank and pray to Him, beg His forgiveness, receive His Body and Soul, see and hear Him, and accept the promised gifts of His Holy Spirit. In other words, this Brother and Savior Jesus Christ lives and breathes in the Church.

The first stage of Christian discipleship, that Jesus is our Brother and Savior, is fairly straight-forward. Jesus is our Brother because we have the same Father, the same One we invoke in the Lord's Prayer. And Jesus is our Savior because our Father sent Him into our world to free us from all our sins, fears, the sting of death and eternal oblivion. So Jesus is our Brother and Savior thanks to the love of our Father, Who, after all, created us and our world.

Once a person, teen or otherwise, truly believes that Jesus is his/her Brother and Savior, the natural question becomes: Where can I go to meet Him? Now, there are many possible places for such an encounter. For a soldier it may be in a foxhole of the battlefield. For a contemplative type it may be a quiet spot on the beach or a scenic mountainside. It might even be a hospital room, a jail cell or the cozy confines of one's own den. But the surest place to encounter the Lord, as proven by the experience of millions during the last two millennia, is in the company of one's brothers and sisters in church. Youth ministers, both lay and clergy, simply must demonstrate to the young generation that the church is THE place, the MAIN place to meet Jesus Christ, our Brother and Savior. The church is where the youth most assuredly can form and maintain a life-long relationship with Our Lord.

It is one thing to gather up the youth in the church, but it's a totally different thing to keep them there. The old adage about leading a horse to water comes to mind. Demographers refer to this "keeping them there" as Retention. Fortunately, we know exactly how this retention can be accomplished with three simple practices.

The first practice every serious pastor should employ is a welcoming committee at every church entrance. These folks should be instructed to greet all comers in the language "de jour", whether English or Spanish, Italian or Polish. It is really effective to have these greeters positioned both inside and outside the entry-way, as they pass out the weekly church bulletin. But the real key here to attract the youth is to have young people performing this ministry. It is no big secret that teens and early twenties love nothing more than to meet other teens and early twenties. And the older folks will marvel: "Wow, look at all these young people". As quickly as you can say "benvenuto" or "vitaymo", the old lament heard in so many parishes "Where are all the young people?" will disappear.

Young people the world over love music. That's a fact! If a parish hopes to retain the youth in the pews, it simply must have good music at the Mass or Liturgy Whether rock or rap, country or western, classical or pop, young people will go anywhere, to fill any venue (and pay any price!) to listen, and, more importantly, sing along to their favorite music. A church without good and rousing music is dead, pure and simple, in the minds of youth today. In such a church the pastor and parent alike hear that dreaded word "boring" from the teens as their reason for staying home.

This second necessary practice of celebrating services with powerful and moving music can be accomplished in choral or congregational form with the priest or deacon at the altar. But the entire congregation must be drawn into the music and urged to sing along. The old Latin adage is as true today as it was for the Medievals: "He who sings, prays twice."

In the Eastern Churches, Catholic and Orthodox, virtually all the divine services are to be sung. Basically, the priest or deacon sings the given prayer and the faithful respond musically. All the singing is done without instrumentation in mostly antiphonal mode. Two young Mexicans, Jose and Bianca were married in our Church last year with about thirty young friends and family in attendance. When Father Pastor chanted the Great Ektenia with its 12 petitions, the faithful responded in perfect harmony "Signor, ten piedad" (Lord, have mercy"). The mood in the church became instantly heavenly, as if God's angels had descended to sing the nuptial prayers for this young Hispanic couple.

Singing is magical, mystical and emotional. It reaches the very depth of one's soul to comfort and elevate the heart and mind to the higher and greater things in life. Religion without singing is usually dull and lifeless. In a very real sense, it is either sing or go home for today's Church.

The third practice that needs attention in order to retain not only the youth in church, but the faithful of all ages, is preaching. Father Andrew Greeley, the late Chicago author and sociologist, made a virtual living complaining about the poor quality of preaching in the Church today. Our observation is that there are few "Billy Grahams" or "Fulton Sheens" gracing the pulpits of our churches today. Most clergy are fair to middling preachers. Not much charisma is evident in these homilists.

A local Roman Catholic Church was served for fifteen years by a curate from the Far East. An audible groan would arise from the faithful every Sunday when the good Father climbed the pulpit, for the pew-sitters knew what was coming: 30 minutes of unintelligible repetition with literally 100's of "you knows". In contrast, the local Baptist minister, a youngish Ukrainian fellow from North Jersey, delivers a powerful and stirring message every Sunday that is met with thunderous "Amens". As a result the Baptist church registers two or three new families every week, mostly former Catholics.

Greeting, singing and preaching are the hallmarks of a successful parish church. You can bet you last "Benjamin" that if there is a vibrant and growing church in your area, the faithful are made to feel welcome there, their spirits are made to soar musically and their hearts are filled with a powerful message of the Gospel.

Today's youth yearn to be welcomed into our religious communities. Music is their means to connect to the wide world. And they deserve to hear the salvific message of Jesus Christ in a clear and spirited way. This is precisely what your parish and mine should and could be.

Christ loved the youth. The teacher ("Rabbi" is Hebrew) in Him even invited a handful of young men to be His first students and emissaries to the world when he returned home to heaven. The Church simply must follow His example to gather up the youth, teach them the holy mission of the Master and send them out into the world as His disciples.

EPILOGUE

A s a young priest in graduate school, I was stricken with a fairly common malady known as clericalitis. The presented symptoms included the "Father knows best" syndrome, which translates as the priest knows more than any layman about teaching, preaching, organizing, administering, fund-raising and all related practices. The more degrees I earned, including a doctorate, the worse the symptoms became. Until, one day, I met Bill Graham, the legendary head of the Speech and Drama Department of the Catholic University of America. I took his course with just a handful of others and soon discovered, in an ego-busting shock, that I knew next to nothing about the communication sciences. This married layman "took me to school", literally, in the area of human communication. This experience way back then taught me the main lesson and theme of this book, namely, that if the Church is to survive in any recognizable form, it simply must empower the talented laity to share in its main ministry of communicating the Gospel of Jesus Christ.

Another lesson learned from almost fifty years of ministry in the sacred Vineyard is to be straight and upfront with the faithful. A few decades ago I agonized for months over the near-bankrupt status of a small parish I served. Bills were going unpaid, collections were down and the proverbial wolf was at the rectory door. I finally overcame my shame and priestly pride and broke the sad news to the Bishop and the faithful, as well as the neighboring clergy. Instantly, help began to arrive in the form of loans, gifts, pledges and even moral support. In no time at all the little parish was back in the black and my nerve pills found a new home in the trash basket. I learned, then and there, that the faithful not only can be informed but should be told of the crises, problems and difficulties in the Church. They will not only understand but most often help find a solution. Churchmen simply must swallow their pride, admit their failures and appeal for support from the laity. Once the clergy tell the truth to the world, this selfsame truth will set the Church free to carry on the mission of Jesus the Christ.

The final theme of our work concerns the role of women in the Church. For some 1900 years now the Church has been a male-operated and male-oriented institution. It can be argued that this situation simply mirrors the reality of the Western World's society in general. But the Church should be above and beyond secular society in its vision and values. It is sadly sobering to remember that only within the last generation or so has the Church been graced with female acolytes and Eucharistic ministers, as well as female Chancery staffers and participants in the Holy Thursday foot-washing ritual. One would think that an institution that bars half its population from any leadership and decision-making roles would be vastly improved with an all-inclusion policy? It certainly is high time to at least consider the appointment of female cardinals, chancellors, finance and HR board members.

There is absolutely no doubt that today's Church is facing huge problems and unprecedented challenges, as we described above. There is also no doubt that the laity, especially women and youth, can provide much needed leadership and wisdom in solving these crises, if given a chance. And I personally have no doubt that Our Lord Himself, as well as His newly appointed Vicar in Rome, Pope Francis, would smilingly bless such an initiative. The Marthas and Marys of the 21st century are ready and quite able to serve. They just need an invitation.

CPSIA information can be obtained at www.ICGtesting.com
Printed in the USA
LVOW04s0635200315

431216LV00002B/56/P